S. HRG. 114–63

THE CURRENT STATE OF READINESS OF U.S. FORCES IN REVIEW OF THE DEFENSE AUTHORIZATION REQUEST FOR FISCAL YEAR 2016 AND THE FUTURE YEARS DEFENSE PROGRAM

HEARING

BEFORE THE

COMMITTEE ON ARMED SERVICES
UNITED STATES SENATE

ONE HUNDRED FOURTEENTH CONGRESS

FIRST SESSION

MARCH 25, 2015

Printed for the use of the Committee on Armed Services

Available via the World Wide Web: http://www.fdsys.gov/

U.S. GOVERNMENT PUBLISHING OFFICE

96–067 PDF   WASHINGTON : 2015

For sale by the Superintendent of Documents, U.S. Government Publishing Office
Internet: bookstore.gpo.gov   Phone: toll free (866) 512–1800; DC area (202) 512–1800
Fax: (202) 512–2104   Mail: Stop IDCC, Washington, DC 20402–0001

COMMITTEE ON ARMED SERVICES

JOHN McCAIN, Arizona, *Chairman*

JAMES M. INHOFE, Oklahoma
JEFF SESSIONS, Alabama
ROGER F. WICKER, Mississippi
KELLY AYOTTE, New Hampshire
DEB FISCHER, Nebraska
TOM COTTON, Arkansas
MIKE ROUNDS, South Dakota
JONI ERNST, Iowa
THOM TILLIS, North Carolina
DAN SULLIVAN, Alaska
MIKE LEE, Utah
LINDSEY GRAHAM, South Carolina
TED CRUZ, Texas

JACK REED, Rhode Island
BILL NELSON, Florida
CLAIRE McCASKILL, Missouri
JOE MANCHIN III, West Virginia
JEANNE SHAHEEN, New Hampshire
KIRSTEN E. GILLIBRAND, New York
RICHARD BLUMENTHAL, Connecticut
JOE DONNELLY, Indiana
MAZIE K. HIRONO, Hawaii
TIM KAINE, Virginia
ANGUS S. KING, JR., Maine
MARTIN HEINRICH, New Mexico

CHRISTIAN D. BROSE, *Staff Director*
ELIZABETH L. KING, *Minority Staff Director*

(II)

CONTENTS

MARCH 25, 2015

Page

(III)

THE CURRENT STATE OF READINESS OF U.S. FORCES IN REVIEW OF THE DEFENSE AUTHORIZATION REQUEST FOR FISCAL YEAR 2016 AND THE FUTURE YEARS DEFENSE PROGRAM

WEDNESDAY, MARCH 25, 2015

U.S. SENATE
SUBCOMMITTEE ON READINESS AND
MANAGEMENT SUPPORT,
COMMITTEE ON ARMED SERVICES
Washington, DC.

The subcommittee met, pursuant to notice, at 2:34 p.m. in room SR–232A, Russell Senate Office Building, Senator Kelly Ayotte (chairman of the subcommittee) presiding.

Committee members present: Senators Ayotte, Rounds, Kaine and Shaheen.

OPENING STATEMENT OF SENATOR KELLY AYOTTE, CHAIRMAN

Senator AYOTTE. I'm going to call this hearing to order.

Very much want to thank our distinguished witnesses who are here before us today who have so admirably served our Nation.

This hearing of the Subcommittee on Readiness and Management Support will be the second hearing of the year to receive testimony on the current readiness of our military forces.

I want to thank my Ranking Member, Senator Kaine, for his continued leadership on defense issues and his eagerness to work together in a bipartisan manner for the sake of our national security.

We are joined this afternoon with a very distinguished panel. We are here with General Daniel Allyn, Vice Chief of Staff of the Army; Admiral Michelle Howard, Vice Chief of Staff of Naval Operations; General John Paxton, Vice Commandant of the Marine Corps; and General Larry Spencer, Vice Chief of Staff for the Air Force.

Again, I don't think we can say enough about what a tremendous group of leaders that we have testifying before this committee today. I cannot think of a more important hearing topic for this committee than the readiness of our Armed Forces.

The preeminent responsibility of the Federal Government is to provide for the common defense. In order to fulfill this foundational responsibility of our Government, Congress has been explicitly charged, in Article 1, Section 8, of the Constitution, with the authority and responsibility to raise and support armies, and provide

(1)

and maintain the Navy. We have to begin with an objective assessment of our national security interests and the threats that we're facing around the world. We then should determine what defense capabilities and capacities we need in order to protect our interests against likely threats. That is how you develop a defense budget that keeps America safe.

Unfortunately, that's not what we have been seeing with the impact of sequester in Washington. Rather than a reality-based, strategy-based defense budgets, we are seeing that the impact of sequester is deeply disconnected from the many threats that we face around the world right now. In fact, in testimony before the Armed Services Committee earlier this year, the Director of National Intelligence (DNI), James Clapper, I think summed up the current situation very well. He said, ''In my 50-plus years in the intelligence business, I don't know of a time that has been more beset by challenges and crises around the world. As these threats have grown in complexity and severity, the defense budget cuts have created a growing and troubling gap between the military we need and the military our national security interests require. The consequences of failing to address this are grave.''

It's easy for us in Washington to lose sight of the real-world consequences of our decisions. We all know that the readiness of our forces is something that we don't often see, but we'll know right away if it's not there, given what we ask of our men and women of uniform.

When we send our fellow citizens into harm's way, they rely on us to provide them with the best possible training and equipment so that they can accomplish their missions and return home safely. I think not only do we have a constitutional obligation to do so, we have a moral obligation to do so. I know the witnesses before me appreciate that better than anyone.

That's why I look forward to continuing to work across the aisle with people like my Ranking Member to address the sequestration, because we do need to come up with a bipartisan solution to this in the long term so that we can make the right decisions today by our men and women in uniform and to ensure that we are prepared to face the grave threats that, unfortunately, are unfolding around the world.

Before I go to my Ranking Member, you know, I know that many of my colleagues right now are having a meeting with President Ghani, the President of Afghanistan, who just finished a joint address to the Congress. Having been present for that address, I think that he, the President, first of all, made very clear the gratitude that the leader of Afghanistan has for the sacrifices that our men and women in uniform have made to help ensure the security of Afghanistan. But, what we also heard is what a difference our men and women in uniform have made in Afghanistan, and appreciate the difference we have made throughout the world, and particularly when he talked about the freedom with which he believes women should have in Afghanistan and the fact that, before our presence in Afghanistan, not one girl went to school.

So, I want to bring this up, because we need to understand there is no other leader in the world like the United States of America. If we do not continue to invest in the best military in the world, then we will not be prepared for the challenges we face, but also the world will be a much worse place and a much more dangerous place without our assistance.

I want to—in that regard, I wanted to mention, since we have the President of Afghanistan here, that there has been a report, unfortunately, that today there were 6 people killed and more than 30 wounded in a suicide bombing in Kabul, right near the presidential palace. So, I think it reminds us that dangers still remain there, and that they remain many places around the world. So, your testimony today is so important.

I would like to turn this over to my Ranking Member.

STATEMENT OF SENATOR TIM KAINE

Senator KAINE. Great. Thank you, Madam Chair.

I echo your comments. It's good to work together on these issues. We have a bipartisan working relationship and, I think, a common understanding of the dangers of sequester.

Could they just give us the budget for 15 minutes, just the two of us, and—we can hammer this out.

Senator AYOTTE. We could do it.

[Laughter.]

Senator AYOTTE. We really could work this out.

Senator KAINE. Let me start with the thank you that Chairman Ayotte was talking about with respect to the speech from the Afghan President this morning. If you were—I wish you were there. I hope you watched it. It should make you feel really proud. You know, it made me feel proud on your behalf, but you should feel proud, and you should feel proud for your folks, because the notion of a country—I'll just pick one statistic—that's gone from a 44-year-old life expectancy to a 61- or 62-year-old life expectancy in 15 years, I mean, it—there's just no precedent in human history for that. I have been doing my back-of-the-envelope calculation. Seventeen years of human life multiplied by 30 million Afghans is 510 million years of human life. That's what the U.S. has enabled them to achieve, because they didn't have a functioning health system, and it was a whole lot of non-governmental organizations (NGOs) who came in and helped set it up, but they couldn't set it up if the security situation didn't enable them to. So, the U.S. and partners, working together with the Afghan people, have created a situation where, violence notwithstanding, challenges notwithstanding, kids are in school, there's a new sense of optimism and hope, people are living longer. As the President said, for the kids that are in school, their parents thank you. For the people who are living longer, their children thank you. He did that in a very poetic way that was really special.

So, look, but it also means that the work doesn't end. You can't stop the investment. We've got to continue the partnership. That partnership demands a military that's ready.

We've had a series of hearings—this is the second one of this subcommittee, but others—where we've talked about sequester. Madam Chair, we had one this morning in the Seapower Subcommittee, where this was the testimony. The Seapower hearing this morning, chaired by Senator Wicker and Ranking Member Hirono, dealt with the naval and marine aviation platforms. That was the hearing. But, they were talking about the triple whammy of sequester. So, here's the triple whammy of sequester on this kind of component of readiness. Sequester and budget caps slows down the ability to purchase new platforms. So, since we can't purchase the new platforms we need, let's extend the life of existing platforms, let's take planes that were meant to fly 6,000 hours and make them fly 10,000 hours. Well, to do that, you've got to do a lot of maintenance. Since the planes weren't supposed to fly after 6,000 hours, you find a whole lot of challenging maintenance problems with planes that have been in saltwater environments, corrosion because of saltwater, or have been in desert environments, corrosion because of sand—so then there's a whole lot of extra depot and maintenance demand that we didn't necessarily plan for. Oh, by the way, because we furloughed a whole lot of employees and stuff, and great aviation mechanics can get jobs elsewhere, we're down about 10 percent of what we need in the workforce.

So, sequester stopped us on the—slowed us on the new purchases. Sequester is imposing significant extra demands on the maintenance of these aircraft. Sequester is driving away some of our workforce. Yet, we are supposed to, nevertheless, do the mission that the Nation demands. Then you add to it the Chairwoman's comment from DNI Clapper, ''This is the most complex strategic set of challenges we see,'' readiness is not happening in a vacuum. Readiness is happening after our military has been at Operational Tempo (Ops Tempo) for 15 years. That, in and of itself—forget about sequester—that has a readiness challenge to it.

So, you combine 15 years of Ops Tempo and a complex strategic environment and the budgetary challenges of caps and across-the-board cuts and furloughs and then sort of the uncertainty, ''Is Congress going to fix it, or not?'' and you can see why we have such a huge budgetary challenge that we have to resolve.

Retired General Mattis, at a hearing earlier this year, said, ''No foe could wreak such havoc on our security as mindless sequestration is achieving.'' No foe could wreak such havoc on our security as mindless sequestration is achieving.

If a large-scale conflict were to occur in the near future, Armed Forces would not have enough ready forces to respond to the Combatant Command (COCOM) requirements, we'd likely suffer additional casualties as a result. We've had that testimony.

So, this has been like an alarm bell that's just been ringing, you know, on our table next to us. Your testimony, combined testimony, has been like the alarm bell's been ringing, ringing, ringing, ringing, ringing. There just has to be a moment where we take a step to turn off the alarm and adjust to a better path. In the fiscal year 2014 and 2015 budget, we were able to find a way to reduce the impact of sequester—not eliminate it, cut it in half. It may be pie in the sky to think we could eliminate it. But, we ought to be finding significant sequester relief, whether it's depot maintenance or extra plane hours or the effect on the workforce that furloughs create, in terms of morale for people who have other opportunities. All these are significant.

That's what we'll be hearing about during the testimony today. I look forward to working with my colleagues trying to find, based on your testimony, and based on your—you know, giving us the stories and the anecdotes we need to convince our colleagues, I look forward to trying to find a better path.

With that, thank you, Madam Chair.

Senator AYOTTE. Thank you, Senator Kaine.

I would like to first call on General Allyn, the Vice Chief of Staff for the Army.

Thank you, General.

STATEMENT OF GENERAL DANIEL B. ALLYN, USA, VICE CHIEF OF STAFF, UNITED STATES ARMY

General ALLYN. Thank you, Chairman Ayotte, Ranking Member Kaine, Senator Rounds, distinguished members of the subcommittee. Thank you for the opportunity to testify on the readiness of your United States Army.

On behalf of our Secretary, The Honorable John McHugh, and our Chief of Staff, General Ray Odierno, I thank you for your support and demonstrated commitment to our soldiers, Army civilians, families, and veterans.

There are over 140,000 soldiers committed around the globe, partnered with our allies, in response to increasing instability across Europe, the Middle East, Africa, and the Pacific, continuing the mission in Afghanistan, and reacting to humanitarian crises. The velocity of instability is increasing, as you have all stated; and now is not the time to drastically reduce our capability or capacity. The Army needs Congress to provide adequate, consistent, and predictable funding.

Today, only 33 percent of our brigades are ready, when our sustained readiness rate should be closer to 70 percent. The fiscal year '15 enacted funding for our Army is $5.1 billion less than what we had in fiscal year 2014 and challenges commanders and leaders across our Army to sustain hard-fought gains in our readiness. We are funded to achieve just enough readiness for immediate consumption, but are unable to generate the readiness required to respond to an unknown contingency.

While the fiscal year 2015 budget constrains training, we remain committed to our Combat Training Center rotations to develop leaders and build unit readiness. We accept risk in home-station training to conserve resources for these Combat Training Center rotations. The result of this approach is that we expect our units to arrive at our Combat Training Centers not fully ready for these complex training scenarios and, therefore, unable to derive the full benefit of this training.

Under the President's Budget in fiscal year 2016 (PB–16), our goal is to increase regular Army brigade combat team readiness closer to 70 percent, allowing us to balance force requirements while maintaining surge capability. But, we need consistent resources to get there.

Sequestration will undermine readiness, ultimately putting soldiers' lives and our mission success at risk, and it will increase significantly the involuntary separation of officer and noncommissioned officer leaders who have steadfastly served their country through the last 13 years of war. Sequestration will also severely impact our ability to maintain our installation readiness and protect the industrial base, both key components to maintaining a readiness—a ready force. It will cut essential funds from military construction, sustainment, restoration, and modernization on our installations. Sequestration will degrade the industrial base's ability to sustain the life-cycle readiness of warfighting equipment while also maintaining the capability to surge to meet future demands.

To achieve our required readiness level in fiscal year '16, we need Congress to support all the cost-saving measures the Army has proposed. These include compensation reform, a new round of Base Realignment and Closure, and the Aviation Restructure Initiative (ARI). Aviation restructure eliminates 700 aircraft from the Active component and 111 from the Guard and Reserve, but increases our readiness and saves $12 billion. If the Army does not execute ARI, we will incur additional costs buying aircraft and performing maintenance, at the expense of modernizing our systems and maintaining readiness for our heroic aviators.

The Army remains committed to protecting our most important resource: our soldiers, civilians, and families. We build leaders of character and trusted professionals who provide an environment where every member of our great Army is treated with dignity and respect, supported by essential soldier and family programs. We will protect our most vital programs, but sequestration-driven budget cuts affect every facet of our Army.

I thank you again for your steadfast support of the outstanding men and women of the United States Army. I look forward to your questions.

Thank you.

[The prepared statement of General Allyn follows:]

PREPARED STATEMENT BY GENERAL DANIEL ALLYN, VICE CHIEF OF STAFF UNITED STATES ARMY

INTRODUCTION

Chairman Ayotte, Ranking Member Kaine, distinguished Members of the Subcommittee, thank you for the opportunity to testify on the readiness of your United States Army. On behalf of our Secretary, the Honorable John McHugh, and our Chief of Staff, General Raymond Odierno, I would also like to thank you for your support and demonstrated commitment to our Soldiers, Army Civilians, Families, and Veterans.

We live in a dangerous world and the Leadership of the United States Army is committed to ensuring our Army is ready. The accelerating insecurity and instability across Europe, the Middle East, Africa and the Pacific, coupled with the continued threat to the homeland and our ongoing operations in Afghanistan, remain a significant focus for our Army. The Islamic State in Iraq and the Levant's (ISIL) unforeseen expansion and the rapid disintegration of order in Iraq and Syria have dramatically escalated conflict in the region. In Europe, Russia's intervention in Ukraine violates international law and threatens to undermine the post-World War II security architecture. Across the Asia-Pacific, China's lack of transparency regarding its military modernization efforts raises concerns with the United States and our allies, and the continuing development of North Korea's nuclear and missile programs contributes to instability. The rate of complex-humanitarian requirements and the unpredictable nature of disaster relief missions heighten the level of uncertainty we face around the world, along with constantly evolving threats to the homeland. With the velocity of instability increasing around the world and the threat of terrorism growing rather than receding, now is not the time to drastically reduce capability and capacity that would occur under prolonged sequestration level-funding.

As the Chief of Staff of the Army stated in his testimony, there is a growing divide between the emerging geopolitical realities and the Budget Control Act's (BCA) arbitrary funding mechanism. The Army budget has decreased in nominal terms every year since 2011. Yet today, the Army is as globally engaged as ever, with more than 140,000 Soldiers deployed, forward stationed, and committed worldwide. We are training alongside our allies and partners to help them develop professional and capable armies. At home, we are supporting civil authorities while defending our critical networks against cyber attacks. Yet prolonged funding at BCA levels prevents us from appropriately balancing readiness, modernization and end strength, and threatens to make the Army a hollow force. Under sequestration-level funding, the Army will be unable to meet its current target for regaining full-spectrum readiness by fiscal year 2023.

Our Nation requires a trained and ready Army prepared to rapidly deploy, fight, sustain itself and win decisively against complex state and non-state threats in diverse, austere environments, rugged terrain and urban megacities. Readiness is measured at both the service and unit level. Service readiness incorporates installations and the critical ability of the Army to provide requisite capabilities in support of the Joint Force in sufficient capacity to execute the missions required by combatant commands. Unit readiness is the combination of personnel, materiel and supplies, equipment and training, that, when properly balanced, enables immediate and effective application of military power.

To ensure readiness now and in the future, the Army needs Congress to provide adequate, consistent and predictable funding. The Army supports the President's Budget as meeting the required funding and needed reforms to fulfill our responsibilities defined in the Defense Strategic Guidance. One critical assumption in the President's Budget request is that Congress will enact critical cost saving measures we have proposed. These include compensation reform, sustainable energy and resource initiatives, a new round of Base Realignments and Closure (BRAC), and the Aviation Restructure Initiative (ARI). We ask Congress to support these initiatives because without the flexibility to manage our budgets to achieve the greatest capability possible, we will be forced to make even steeper reductions to manpower, modernization, and training across the Total Army.

Current State of Readiness

Thirteen years of sustained counterinsurgency-focused operations have degraded the Army's ability to conduct operations across the entire spectrum of war. In fiscal year 2011, the Army began a multi-year transition to rebuild core readiness and build capability to conduct Decisive Action for Unified Land Operations. The speed and scale of the funding reductions mandated under sequestration in fiscal year 2013 curtailed this transition plan by forcing the Army to absorb the majority of the cuts within the operations and training accounts. This resulted in tiered readiness of units as opposed to broad gains across the force.

Last year the Chief of Staff of the Army testified that only two of our Brigade Combat Teams, the Army's basic warfighting unit, were fully ready for decisive action operations. Since then, we have trained 13 BCTs to that standard (other CTC rotations were mission-specific for deploying units) thanks to funding provided in the 2013 Bipartisan Budget Agreement (BBA). However, of those 13 BCTs, we have consumed the readiness of nine to support on-going operations. At prolonged sequestration-level funding, the Army will be unable to train units quickly enough to outpace, or even meet demand.

With the support of Congress, the Army executed $126.2 billion for base budget purposes in fiscal year 2014 to begin rebuilding readiness lost during sequestration in fiscal year 2013. Though known and predictable, the fiscal year 2015-enacted level of $121 billion is $5.1 billion less than fiscal year 2014, and is challenging Commanders across the Army to sustain our hard-earned readiness. To operate under this budget, we are significantly reducing key installation services, individual training events, and modernization to such an extent as to jeopardize future readiness and quality of life. For example, Logistics Readiness Centers were underfunded by $350 million in fiscal year 2015, which covers funding for dining facilities, contract operations at ammo supply points, central issue facilities, maintenance, laundry and dry cleaning operations. In addition to the effect on Soldier quality of life, these cuts force Commanders to divert Soldiers from training to perform logistics tasks.

The President's Budget request for fiscal year 2016 increases readiness funding above fiscal year 2015 levels, which is critical to sustain and improve the readiness of the force. While the reduced fiscal year 2015 budget will reduce overall training, we remain committed to CTC rotations to develop leaders and build unit readiness. fiscal year 2015 plans fund 19 CTC rotations: two for deploying BCTs and 17 decisive action rotations (15 Active Army and two Army National Guard). fiscal year 2016 will continue this level of CTC exercises.

We are improving Training Support Systems to enable more realistic home station training, increase collective training proficiency and enhance operational readiness for contingencies across the globe; however, funding constraints in fiscal year 2015 impede our ability to maximize home station training goals. We accepted risk in home station training to conserve resources for units to continue to conduct training at the CTCs. This resulted in units arriving at the CTCs not yet "fully ready" for these complex training scenarios, and therefore unable to derive the full benefit of the training. Although the Army attempts to mitigate the impacts on training readiness, we must continue to implement the Contingency Force model of fiscal year 2015 in order to maintain readiness for the 24 of 60 BCTs that will receive sufficient funding to conduct training at CTCs and home station. The remaining 36 BCTs will train only to Individual/Crew/Squad resourcing levels. The President's Budget request for fiscal year 2016 allows the Army to increase training readiness to battalion-level across the active Component force and to platoon-level in the Reserves. Lower funding levels will not allow us to achieve this balanced readiness.

Our aim is to provide tough, realistic multi-echelon home-station training using a mix of live, virtual and constructive methods that efficiently and effectively build Soldier, leader and unit competence over time. Training will integrate the unique capabilities of the Light, Medium and Heavy forces, as well as the capabilities of Conventional and Special Operations Forces. Training centers including the Joint Multinational Readiness Center in Germany will increase our interoperability with Allies. Our goal is to achieve a high level of readiness for 70 percent of our Active Component BCTs compared to the current 33 percent, allowing the Army to balance Combatant Command force requirements while maintaining surge capability – but we need consistent resources to get there.

We are also increasing funding for our individual and institutional training. Funding increases focus on leader development, entry-level training and flight training. The unpredictable nature of human conflict requires leaders ready to lead in close combat and to understand the operational and strategic environment, including its socio-economic, cultural and religious underpinnings. Junior leaders will frequently confront ethical dilemmas, with resultant decisions that have strategic impacts. Our leaders must demonstrate the competence and professional values necessary to achieve operational and strategic mission success.

However, sequestration in fiscal year 2016 would mortgage the functional skills and training of individual Soldiers. Sequestration will force the Army to further reduce Specialized Skill Training by over 85,000 seats (65 percent drop) and fund only the most critical courses. This will reduce readiness as Soldiers will lose proficiency on their individual tasks. These reductions include 900 fewer graduate flight school seats, resulting in unfilled and unqualified pilot positions throughout the force. We would continue to emphasize leader development by protecting Professional Military Education, minimizing cuts to about 10 percent.

The Army continues to make progress at integrating the unique capabilities of each of its components to support the needs of the Combatant Commanders. As part of the Army's Total Force Policy, the U.S. Army Forces Command is leading the way by partnering Guard and Reserve divisions and brigades with Active Army peer units. The Army is also piloting a program to assign Guard and Reserve personnel directly to Active Army corps and division headquarters. For example, the Reserve Component rapidly provided support capabilities to Operation United Assistance in Liberia to augment and replace elements of the initial Active Component response. We fight as a Total Army, and each component has a unique role. We must also draw down as a Total Army—Active, Guard, and Reserve—in order to maintain the correct balance between capacity and readiness.

As we transition from combat operations in Afghanistan, our Army is focused on the ability to rapidly deploy forces around the world in order to meet the needs of our Combatant Commanders. To do this, we enhanced prepositioned equipment sets and created activity sets to support operations in Europe, the Pacific and around the world. Activity sets are prepositioned arrays of equipment that enable U.S. regionally-aligned forces and multinational partners in Europe to train and operate. We have also reinvigorated our Emergency Deployment Readiness Exercise program and enhanced the en route mission command capability of our Global Response Force. The President's Budget request provides sufficient capability to respond in each Geographical Combatant Command's area of responsibility.

The Army continues to be a good steward of the resources returning from operations in Afghanistan. In 2014, the Army efficiently synchronized equipment retrograde out of theater. Redeployment and retrograde operations remain on schedule; however, the Army continues to forecast a need for reset funding for three years after redeployment of the last piece of equipment from theater. In addition, we identified almost $2 billion of potential requirement reductions in Contractor Logistics and Training Support. These and other changes allowed the Army to increase the capability of its prepositioned stocks program without an increase in associated costs.

Finally, during this period of drawdown, the Army is reorganizing, realigning and restructuring forces. The Brigade Combat Team reorganization enhances brigade combat power by adding a third maneuver battalion to 38 BCTs by the end of fiscal year 2015 and reducing the total number of BCTs to 60 (32 Active Army and 28 Army National Guard) in the Total Force. This effort decreases the number of headquarters units and personnel without negatively affecting the number of operational battalions.

Since May 2014, we have been developing a sustainable force generation and readiness model to account for the new, volatile, strategic operating environment and the need to remain regionally-engaged under budgetary and force-sizing realities. The Sustainable Readiness Model (SRM) will provide force generation policies and processes that optimize the readiness of the force and balance the Army's steady state missions, contingency response capability, and available resources. We cannot predict the specific events that will cause the next surge in demand for Army forces, but history suggests it will come sooner than we expect. The SRM will better enable the future smaller force to sustain readiness at optimal levels over time.

One critical assumption in the President's Budget request is that Congress will enact necessary compensation reform and force structure initiatives. We fully support the modest reforms to pay raises, health care and other benefits that have been proposed. Without these reforms, savings assumptions we have included in our planning will not be realized, placing increasing pressure on further end strength reductions and reducing funding needed to sustain readiness.

Future Readiness: The Army Operating Concept

While we are most concerned about the BCT's short-term effects on readiness, we are keenly focused on the long-term readiness of the Total Force to meet future demands. As such, we developed a new Army Operating Concept (AOC), ''Win in a Complex World.'' The AOC provides an intellectual framework for learning and for applying what we learn to future force development under Force 2025 and Beyond. The foundation of the Army Operating Concept is our ability to conduct joint combined arms maneuver. The Army Operating Concept endeavors to build a force capable of operating alongside multiple partners, able to create multiple dilemmas for our adversaries, while giving our Senior Leaders multiple options and synchronizing and integrating effects from multiple domains onto and from land. Recognizing the changing world around us, the Army Operating Concept envisions an Army that is expeditionary, tailorable, scalable and prepared to meet the challenges of the global environment. The Army Operating Concept sets the foundation upon which our leaders can focus our efforts and resources to maintain strategic and operational flexibility to deter and operate in multiple regions simultaneously − in all phases of military operations − to prevent conflict, shape the security environment, and win wars now and in the future.

It is imperative that our Army adapts to the future joint operating environment, one that consists of diverse enemies that employ traditional, irregular and hybrid strategies which threaten U.S. security and vital interests. Through a dedicated ''Campaign of Learning'' under Force 2025 Maneuvers, we will assess new capabilities, force designs, and doctrine to ensure the readiness of our future force. We are focusing our innovation efforts in this Campaign of Learning to address the 20 Army Warfighting Challenges identified in the Army Operating Concept. The Army Warfighting Challenges are enduring first-order problems, and solving them will improve combat effectiveness. They range from shaping the Security Environment, to countering Weapons of Mass Destruction, to conducting Space and Cyber Operations, to Integrating and Delivering Fires, to Exercising Mission Command. The Army Operating Concept represents a long-term, cost-effective way to enhance readiness, improve interoperability and modernize the force.

Installation Readiness

In order to partially mitigate the severe impacts of sequestration-level funding on training readiness, the Army will be forced to take significant risk with installation readiness. Installation maintenance has been underfunded since 2011 which impacts efficiency and readiness. Sequestration in fiscal year 16 would cut essential funds for military construction, sustainment, restoration and modernization on our posts, camps and stations. The President's fiscal year 2016 budget funds 79 percent of the OSD Facility Sustainment Model requirement. Under sequestration the Army would only be able to fund 62 percent of needed repairs, limiting repairs to those needed for life, health, and safety. Restoration and modernization accounts would be underfunded as well. Without relief from sequestration 20 percent of the Army's infrastructure will remain in substandard condition and approximately 100,000 maintenance orders will be deferred each month. Recovery from unfilled maintenance requests will take at least 2–3 years if fully funded and ultimately will affect morale, retention, and readiness.

A return to sequestration-level funding will result in a $1 billion decrease to base operations support, requiring installations to eliminate jobs and scale back or cancel service contracts that employ people in local communities. We will have to increase further our reliance on Soldiers to support basic installation functions in order to provide a safe training environment and adequate quality of life. These include access control point manning by MTOE units, manning ammo and fuel handling points, and conducting essential range maintenance. These requirements pull Soldiers away from important training and ultimately detract from readiness. We will also reduce contract funding for a number of quality-of-life services such as custodial services, waste collection, and grounds maintenance.

It is important to highlight the need for another round of Base Realignment and Closure (BRAC). We simply have too much surplus infrastructure and will have even more as we continue to downsize. We are already in the process of separating nearly 152,000 Soldiers from the Total Army by fiscal year 2018, and sequestration would force us to separate another 60,000 by fiscal year 2020—for a total reduction of 212,000. In addition, we have reduced over 50,000 Civilians from these same installations. Without a BRAC and the realized cost savings, the only alternative is to make additional cuts in training, manpower and modernization to make up for shortages in installation funding. We have reduced all that we can from our overseas bases, and are now reducing personnel at U.S. installations. We expect excess facility capacity will be about 18 percent Army-wide by late fiscal year 2015.

Industrial Base

The Industrial Base consists of Government-owned (organic) and commercial industry and is designed to be readily available to manufacture and repair items during both peacetime and national emergencies. The current financial uncertainty of sequestration, combined with the cuts in Army force structure, is driving workload down. Over 4,500 employees within the organic industrial base (OIB) have already lost their jobs due to budget uncertainty and declining workloads since fiscal year 2013, and the Army has deferred $323 million of depot maintenance from fiscal year 2013 into fiscal year 2015. The highly skilled industrial base workforce serves an enduring mission, and provides critical capabilities in support of our National defense today, while also preparing for the threats of tomorrow. Sequestration will result in insufficient resources to complete critical depot maintenance and will continue to degrade the industrial base's ability to sustain the life-cycle readiness of war-fighting equipment while also maintaining the capability to surge to meet the demands of future contingency operations.

Should sequestration-level funding return in fiscal year 2016, furloughs, overtime restrictions and hiring freezes will again negatively impact the OIB productivity, workforce availability and capability. In order to mitigate the loss of critical skill sets and ensure the OIB is ready for the next contingency, the Army requires consistent and predictable funding. We also need to carryover workload to keep production lines functioning between fiscal years.

The Army is taking several actions to reshape the OIB to support the Army of 2025 and beyond, to include assessing OIB capabilities and capacities and effectively aligning them to planned workloads. We are not sustaining aging systems that are planned for divesture within the next five years, and we are continuing reset and sustainment of our modernized platforms. This strategy will enable the Army to sustain and modernize our most capable fleets, while accomplishing our Title 10 requirements to sustain the core depot and critical manufacturing capabilities necessary to fight and win the Nation's wars.

Aviation Restructure Initiative

One of our most important reforms is the Aviation Restructuring Initiative (ARI), which we continued in fiscal year 2015. Our current aviation structure is unaffordable, so the Army's plan will avoid $12 billion in costs and saves an additional $1 billion annually if we fully implement ARI. We simply cannot afford to maintain our current aviation structure and sustain modernization while providing trained and ready aviation units across all three components. Our comprehensive approach through ARI will ultimately allow us to eliminate obsolete airframes, sustain a modernized fleet, and reduce sustainment costs.

Through ARI, we will eliminate nearly 700 aircraft from the active Component, while removing only 111 airframes in the Reserve Component. A byproduct of ARI is the reduction in the number of Active Duty Combat Aviation Brigades from 13 to 10. ARI eliminates and reorganizes structure, while increasing capabilities in order to minimize risk to meeting operational requirements within the capacity of remaining aviation units across all components. If the Army does not execute ARI, we will incur additional costs associated with buying aircraft and structure at the expense of modernizing current and future aviation systems in the Total Force.

The Army notes the establishment by Congress of a National Commission on the Future of the Army and ARI specifically, and is fully committed to working with the Commission as it fulfills its charter.

Army Cyber

Network dominance and defense is an integral part of our National security, and the Army is focused on providing increased capability to the Joint Force. Investment in cyber capability and readiness is a top priority, and we are working to improve requirements and resourcing processes to ensure that they are agile enough to rapidly translate innovative concepts into realized capabilities. Army readiness includes cyber readiness.

We are aggressively manning, training and equipping cyber mission teams and established a new cyber branch to help recruit, train and retain cyber Soldiers. The Army has grown from zero Cyber teams in fiscal year 2013 to 24 Army Cyber Mission Teams today at Initial Operating Capability (IOC). By the end of fiscal year 2016, we will have 41 Cyber Mission Teams. The Army has established the Cyber Center of Excellence at Fort Gordon, GA, to serve as our focal point to drive change across the Army. This is a Total Force effort—Active, National Guard, and Reserve—and through our Reserve Components we will leverage the professional expertise within the civilian population to build greater capacity, expertise, and flexibility across DOD, Federal, state, and private sector activities. We recently established a full-time Army National Guard Cyber Protection Team (CPT) that is training to conduct network defense. We will create three more Army National Guard CPTs in fiscal year 2016.

We must make prudent investments in our cyber infrastructure, including facilities, networks and equipment to ensure a capable force. Network modernization is critical to the success of Army operations across all domains, and the Army is fully integrated into the build-out of the Joint Information Environment (JIE). JIE efforts will enhance the defensibility of our networks while providing global access for the joint force. However, sequestration-level funding in fiscal year 2016 will reduce network funding by almost $400 million and defer critical scheduled IT infrastructure upgrades at three major installations, reducing the Army's warfighting capability and its ability to protect itself against cyber attacks.

Essential Investments: People and Equipment

Soldiers, Families and Army Civilians

Army Professionalism and the resilience of those who serve—Soldiers, their Families and Army Civilians—are directly linked to the Readiness of our Force. That is why we must develop and sustain a system of capabilities and services that are designed to mitigate the unique challenges of military life, foster life skills, strengthen resilience, and promote a strong and ready Army. As Army leaders, we continue to express our enduring commitment to those who serve, recognizing that attracting and retaining highly-qualified individuals in all three components is critical to readiness. Two of our key efforts, the Army's Ready and Resilient Campaign (R2C) and Soldier for Life, exist to ensure we are taking care of our most precious resource: our people, throughout Army life and beyond.

Ready and Resilient Campaign

We will make every effort to protect our most important Soldier and Family programs, but budget cuts are ultimately affecting every facet of the Army. To ensure we maintain our focus on our most invaluable resource: our people, we continue to develop a Ready and Resilient Army. A Ready and Resilient Army is composed of resilient individuals, adaptive leaders and cohesive teams that are committed to the Army professional ethic and capable of accomplishing a range of operations in environments of uncertainty and persistent danger. We are developing a comprehensive system that empowers Army Commanders and Leaders to improve Leader engagement and early Leader intervention. We are taking a more holistic look at negative behaviors and their correlation in order to better target training, tools and resources with more emphasis placed on resilience and prevention skills to reduce incidents of escalated negative behavioral outcomes.

We continue to provide resilience and performance enhancement training to Soldiers, Families and Army Civilians through Comprehensive Soldier and Family Fitness. To date, we have trained more than 26,000 Master Resilience Trainers Army-wide who are taking these skills back to their formations. We have established an online assessment and self-development platform where Soldiers, their Families and Army Civilians can, in their own time, confidentially take action to improve their overall health and resilience.

We are also emphasizing the importance of sleep, physical activity, and nutrition. The Performance Triad is a comprehensive plan to improve readiness and increase resilience through health initiatives and leadership engagement. Sleep, activity and nutrition are key actions that influence overall health.

Personal Readiness is critical to mission readiness. Those who serve must have the physical, psychological, social, emotional and spiritual preparedness to achieve and sustain optimal performance in supporting the Army mission.

Soldier for Life

Soldier for Life (SFL) is a program that drives a change in mindset. We encourage the SFL mindset through senior leader and installation engagements, and focused training curriculum. We want individuals to understand from their entry day in the Army that they will receive the tools to succeed throughout their service lifecycle – "Once a Soldier, always a Soldier … a Soldier for Life!" As they return to civilian life, Soldiers will continue to influence young people to join the Army and, along with retired Soldiers, will connect communities across the Nation with its Army.

As we reduce the Army's end strength, we owe it to our Soldiers and their Families to facilitate their transition to civilian life. The Army supports continuum of service initiatives to help in this effort by communicating the benefits of continued service in the Reserve Components. Additionally, the "Soldier for Life" Program connects Army, governmental and community efforts to facilitate the successful reintegration of our Soldiers and Families back into communities across the Nation through networks in employment, education and health. Our pre- and post-retirement services ensure those who served become and remain leaders in their community. For example, we have developed strong relationships with government, non-government and private sector entities to include direct collaboration with the Departments of Veterans Affairs, Labor, and the Chamber of Commerce to bring employment summits to installations worldwide.

Sexual Harassment/Assault Response and Prevention (SHARP) Program

Trust between Soldiers, between Soldiers and Leaders, between Soldiers, their Families and the Army, and between the Army and the American people is fundamental to readiness. Sexual assault and sexual harassment undermine that trust.

Across the Army, we are committed to maintaining momentum in Army SHARP and making further advances along our five lines of efforts: Prevention, Investigation, Accountability, Advocacy and Assessment. In the last year, our efforts along the Prevention Line of Effort resulted in actions such as consolidating SHARP training under TRADOC and Initial Entry Training and Professional Military Education to increase the quality and accessibility of our prevention tools. Our Investigation Line of Effort showed advances in Special Victim capabilities and Trial Counsel Assistance Programs. The Accountability Line of Effort had successes through our Special Victim Investigation and Prosecution capability and through tools such as Command Climate Surveys and Commander 360 degree assessments. Our Advocacy Line of Effort resulted in initial indicators of progress in establishing SHARP resource centers for over 12 installations. We continue to see interim progress along our Assessment Line of Effort as noted in the 2014 "Department of Defense Report to the President of the United States on Sexual Assault Prevention and Response."

Recent statistics outlined in the 2014 "DOD Report to the President" indicate a decrease in unwanted sexual contact in fiscal year 2014 compared to fiscal year 2012. Within the Army, survey-estimated rates of unwanted sexual contact for the past year decreased significantly for active duty women (4.6 percent), compared to fiscal year 2012 (7.1 percent). In addition, reporting data demonstrates more victims are coming forward to report sexual harassment and sexual assault. In fiscal year 2014, sexual assault reporting in the Army increased by 12 percent over the previous year. We view this as a vote of confidence and a sign of increased trust. Nevertheless, we must continue striving to foster a climate where individuals are not afraid of retaliation or stigma for reporting a crime by ensuring individuals, units, organizations and specifically commanders and leaders understand their responsibilities. Retaliation takes many forms and originates from many sources—leaders, family, friends and, most pervasively, peer to peer. Retaliation in its simplest form is bullying. It enables offenders, threatens survivors, pushes bystanders to shy from action, and breeds a culture of complacency. Retaliation has no place in the Army and we must stamp it out.

The chain of command must be at the center of any effort to combat sexual assault and harassment, and we must ensure leaders remain fully engaged, involved and vigilant. With commanders at the center of our efforts, we will continue to decrease the prevalence of sexual assault through prevention and encourage greater reporting of the crime.

Sexual assault and sexual harassment will be eliminated when every Soldier, Civilian and Family Member stands up and unequivocally acts to stamp it out. Together, we have an obligation to do all we can to safeguard America's sons and daughters, and maintain trust between Soldiers, Civilians, Families and the Nation. Army leaders, at every level of the chain of command, are doing this through prevention, investigation, accountability, advocacy and assessments.

Modernization

It is impossible to discuss readiness without highlighting modernization, as systems and equipment play a key role in future force readiness. Equipment modernization must address emerging threats in an increasingly sophisticated technological environment. The Army must maintain its ability to contend with such diverse threats as cyber attacks, electronic warfare, unmanned systems, chemical and biological agents, and air and missile threats. Decreases to the Army budget over the past several years significantly impacted Army modernization. Since 2011, the Army has ended 20 programs, delayed 125 and restructured 124. Between 2011 and 2015, Research and Development and Acquisition accounts plunged 35 percent from $31 billion to $20 billion. Procurement alone dropped from $21.3 billion to $13.9 billion. We estimate that sequestration-level funding will affect over 80 Army programs. Major impacts include delays in equipping to support expeditionary forces, delays in combat vehicle and aviation modernization, unaffordable increases in sustainment costs to repair older equipment and increases in capability gaps.

The centerpiece of the Army's Modernization Strategy continues to be the Soldier and the squad. The Army will also develop and field a robust, integrated tactical mission command network linking command posts, and extending out to the tactical edge and across platforms. The Army's objective is to rapidly integrate technologies and applications that empower, protect and unburden the Soldier and our formations, thus providing the Soldier with the right equipment, at the right time, to accomplish the assigned mission.

The President's Budget request would provide over $2 billion to begin to address the growing gaps in our modernization accounts. Even with this additional funding, modernization will require several years to recover from the effects of recent budget reductions and regain balance in the Force. As such, the Army emphasizes early affordability reviews, establishing cost caps (funding and procurement objectives), synchronizing multiple processes and divesting older equipment.

End Strength

Readiness includes possessing the capacity to execute the missions required by the Defense Strategic Guidance and the Combatant Commanders. The minimum end strength the Army requires to fully execute the 2012 Defense Strategic Guidance is 980,000 Soldiers—450,000 in the active Army, 335,000 in the Army National Guard and 195,000 in the Army Reserve. All three components will be smaller than pre-2001 force. If prolonged sequestration-level funding occurs, we will need to reduce end strength even further—to 420,000 in the AC by fiscal year 2020, and 315,000 in the National Guard and 185,000 in the Army Reserve, both by fiscal year 2019. At these levels we assess the Army would be unable to fulfill all the elements of the Defense Strategic Guidance.

Although the Army expects to lose combat-seasoned Soldiers and leaders, our focus through these processes will be on retaining those individuals with the greatest potential for future service in the right grades and with the right skills.

Recap: Effects of Sequestration

At force levels driven by affordability under full sequestration, the Army cannot fully implement its role in the defense strategy. Sequestration would require the Army to further reduce our Total Army end strength to at least 920,000 or 60,000 below the 980,000 currently reflected in the President's Budget request and would severely limit the Army's investment to equip Soldiers to meet the warfighting requirements of tomorrow. Under sequestration-level funding readiness will be reduced to a level the Army will be unable to recover from until well past the current target of fiscal year 2023. Only 24 of 60 Brigade Combat Teams will receive sufficient funding to conduct required readiness training. An estimated 85,000 seats will be lost in specialized skills training, and there will be a $1 billion decrease to base operations support, eliminating jobs, contracts, causing barracks and furnishings to further deteriorate. While we will protect funding for the Combat Training Centers

(CTCs), funding for home station training will be severely reduced which will undermine many units' readiness and inhibit those scheduled for a CTC from adequate preparation.

We are expecting a decline in the overall readiness of our forces because of reduced funding in fiscal year 2015, and sequestration in fiscal year 2016 will dissipate the gains we achieved from the Bipartisan Budget Agreement in fiscal year 2014 and leave the Army in a precarious state. Because we cannot draw down end strength in a rapid manner, operations and training funding would absorb the majority of the budget cuts resulting from sequestration, leaving the Army hollow—lacking training and modern equipment and vulnerable if needed in a crisis. Ultimately, sequestration will put Soldiers' lives at risk.

Closing

As the velocity of instability increases so does the demand for a ready and modern Army, adequately sized and trained to prevent, shape, and win. We ask Congress to repeal the harmful cuts arbitrarily imposed under sequestration-level funding and provide Soldiers with greater predictability in these uncertain times.

We are committed to working closely with Congress to ensure that we are good stewards of our Nation's resources. There are critical cost-saving measures that allow the Army to further reallocate scarce resources to ensure we remain ready and resilient. These include compensation reform, sustainable energy and resource initiatives, a new round of Base Realignment and Closure (BRAC), and the Aviation Restructure Initiative (ARI). We also ask Congress to support a Total Army solution to end strength reductions. Cuts must come from the Total Force – Active, National Guard, and Reserve—to maintain the balance among all components to best execute the Army's strategic mission. We ask Congress to support these initiatives because without the flexibility to manage our budgets to achieve the greatest capability possible, we will be forced to make even larger reductions to manpower, modernization, and training.

The United States Army plays a foundational role in the Joint Force and is indispensible as we work to reassure our allies, deter our enemies, and when necessary, win our Nation's wars. The strength of the All Volunteer Force is our Soldiers, Civilians and their Families, and we must ensure they always stand Ready. History has taught us that the price of improperly managing the readiness of our force will ultimately fall on the backs of our fighting Soldiers. With your assistance, we will continue to resource the best-trained, best-equipped and best-led fighting force in the world. We thank Congress for their steadfast and generous support of the outstanding men and women of the United States Army, our Army Civilians, Families, and Veterans.

Senator AYOTTE. Thank you, General Allyn.

We're now going to hear testimony from Admiral Michelle Howard, who's the Vice Chief of Staff for Naval Operations.

Thank you, Admiral Howard.

STATEMENT OF ADMIRAL MICHELLE J. HOWARD, USN, VICE CHIEF OF NAVAL OPERATIONS, UNITED STATES NAVY

Admiral HOWARD. Chairwoman Ayotte, Senator Kaine, and Senator Rounds, distinguished members of the committee, thank you for the opportunity to testify today.

It is my honor to represent the Navy's Active and Reserve sailors and civilians, and particularly the 41,000 sailors who are underway and deployed around the world today. They're standing watch right now, and ready to meet today's security challenges. The citizens of this Nation can take great pride in the daily contributions of their sons and daughters who fulfill our Navy's longstanding mandate to be where it matters when it matters.

Recent events exemplify the benefit of forward presence. Last August, the *George Herbert Walker Bush* Carrier Strike Group relocated 750 nautical miles from the Arabian Sea to the Arabian Gulf in less than 30 hours. They executed 20 to 30 combat sorties per day. For 54 days, they were the only coalition strike option to project power against the Islamic State of Iraq and Syria (ISIS).

Then there's the U.S.S. *Truxton*, a destroyer that arrived in the Black Sea within a week after Russia invaded Crimea, to help reassure our allies in the area. Another destroyer, U.S.S. *Sampson*, and littoral combat ship U.S.S. *Fort Worth* were among the first vessels to support the search effort for Air Asia Flight 8501 in the Java Sea. Our forward presence truly allows us to be where it matters when it matters.

Effectively operating forward around the globe requires a high state of readiness of our people and platforms. We are still recovering from a degraded readiness as a result of over a decade of combat operations. Sequestration in 2013 exasperated our circumstances and created maintenance backlogs that have prevented us from getting ships back to the fleet on time and aircraft back on the flight line. Since 2013, many ships have been on deployment for 8 to 10 months or longer, negatively impacting the morale of our people and readiness of our ships.

Our Navy fiscal year 2016 budget is designed to continue our readiness recovery, restoring our required contingency operations capacity by the 2018-to-2020 timeframe, while continuing to provide a sustainable forward presence. It also includes credible and survivable sea-based strategic deterrence. With continued overseas operation funding, our fiscal year 2016 budget meets the requirements of the global force management allocation plan. This includes at least two carrier strike groups and two amphibious ready groups operating forward, fully mission capable and certified for deployment.

Recovery of readiness also requires a commitment to protect the time it takes to properly maintain and modernize our capital-intensive force and to conduct full-spectrum training. Achieving full readiness entails the restoration of shipyard capacity and aviation depots primarily through hiring and workforce development, and PB–16 puts us on a path to address these challenges.

I want to make it clear. The Navy's fiscal year 2016 budget is the minimum funding required to execute the Nation's defense strategy. In other words, if we return to a sequestered budget, we will not be able to execute the defense strategic guidance. Past budget shortfalls have forced us to accept significant risks in two important mission areas. The first mission at risk is ''deter and defeat aggression,'' which means to win a war in one theater while deterring another adversary in a different theater. Assuming risk in this mission leads to loss of credibility and ability to assure our allies of our support. The second mission at risk is ''project power despite anti-access aerial-denial challenges.'' This brings risk in our ability to win a war. Some of our people and platforms will arrive late to the fight and inadequately prepared. They will arrive with insufficient ordnance and without the modern combat systems and sensors and networks required to win. Ultimately, this means more ships and aircraft out of action, more sailors, marines, and merchant marines killed.

As we look to the future, the Navy will continue to be globally deployed to provide a credible and survivable strategic deterrent and to support the mission requirements of the regional combatant commanders. The Navy is fundamentally multi-mission and will rapidly adjust to meet new challenges that might require U.S. presence and the—and projecting power.

Our Navy will continue to ensure the security of the maritime domain by sustaining its forward presence, warfighting focus, and readiness preparations. Since there is no foreseeable reduction to global maritime requirements, we have focused our fiscal year Navy budget to address the challenges to achieving the necessary readiness to execute our missions. Any funding below this submission requires a revision of the defense strategy. To put it simply, sequestration will gravely damage the national security of this country. Despite these future challenges, we are fortunate to have the highest quality, the most diverse force in my Navy's history. These outstanding men and women who serve our Nation at sea make us the finest navy in the world.

So, on behalf of all our Active and Reserve sailors, our civilians, and their families, I extend our appreciation to this committee for your efforts and continued support to keep our Navy ready to defend this Nation.

Thank you.

[The prepared statement of Admiral Howard follows:]

PREPARED STATEMENT OF ADMIRAL MICHELLE HOWARD VICE CHIEF OF NAVAL
OPERATIONS ON NAVY READINESS

Chairman Ayotte, Senator Kaine, and distinguished members of the Senate Armed Services Subcommittee on Readiness and Management Support, I appreciate the opportunity to testify on the current state of Navy readiness and the resources necessary to provide a ready Navy in the future as described in our Fiscal Year 2016 budget request. As we meet, the Navy and our sister Services have entered a third year of fiscal uncertainty. In addition, new threats to our nation's interests are emerging and old tensions are surfacing. Today, it is my honor to represent all our active and reserve Sailors, particularly the 41,000 Sailors who are underway on ships and submarines or deployed in expeditionary roles overseas today. They are standing the watch and are ready to meet today's security challenges. American citizens can take great pride in the daily contributions of their sons and daughters who serve in Navy units around the world. We are *where* it matters, *when* it matters, ensuring the security that underpins the global economy and responding to crises.

Last August, the *George H.W. Bush* carrier strike group, already forward present in the North Arabian Sea quickly relocated to the North Arabian Gulf. Flying 20–30 combat sorties per day, this Navy-Marine Corps strike fighter team was the only coalition strike option to project power against the Islamic State of Iraq and the Levant (ISIL) from the skies over Iraq and Syria for 54 days. Similarly, USS *Truxton* (DDG–103) arrived in the Black Sea to establish U.S. presence and to reassure allies a week after Russia invaded Crimea. In the Java Sea, USS *Fort Worth* (LCS–3), a littoral combat ship, and USS *Sampson* (DDG–102), a destroyer, were among the first to support the Indonesian-led search effort for Air Asia Flight 8501. This forward presence is possible because Navy planning and budget decisions continue to be guided by the three tenets the Chief of Naval Operations (CNO) established when he first took office: *Warfighting First, Operate Forward*, and *Be Ready*. Each of these tenets helps drive a strong focus on readiness—both now and in the future.

Actions of Congress helped stabilize readiness by supporting increases over sequestered funding levels through the Bipartisan Budget Act of 2013, and the subsequent authorization and appropriations acts for fiscal year 2014 and this year. Nonetheless, we have not yet recovered from the readiness impact of over a decade of combat operations, exacerbated by the imposition of a lengthy Continuing Resolution and followed by budget sequestration in fiscal year 2013, just as we were beginning to reset the force. These circumstances created maintenance backlogs that have prevented us from getting ships back to the Fleet on time and aircraft back on the flight line. We continue our efforts to rebuild the workforce in our public depots—both shipyards and aviation readiness centers—and reduce the number of lost operational days, but it will take years to dig out of a readiness hole.

The fiscal year 2016 Navy budget submission is designed to continue our readiness recovery, restoring our required contingency operations capacity by 2018–2020 while continuing to provide a sustainable forward presence. PB–16 is the minimum funding required to execute the nation's Defense Strategy, though we still carry risks in two important mission areas, notably when confronted with a technologically advanced adversary or when forced to deny the objective of an opportunistic aggressor in a second region while already engaged in a major contingency. As the CNO stated in his recent testimony to the full committee, risk in our ability to Deter and Defeat Aggression and Project Power Despite Anti-Access/Area Denial (A2/AD) Challenges mean "longer timelines to win, more ships and aircraft out of action in battle, more Sailors, Marines, and Merchant Mariners killed, and less credibility to deter adversaries and assure allies in the future." That level of risk arises from capacity and readiness challenges as well as slower delivery of critical capabilities to the Fleet, particularly in air and missile defense and overall ordnance capacity.

My testimony today will focus on the current readiness of the Navy, and our plan, supported by our fiscal year 2016 budget submission, to meet the challenges to delivering future readiness. If we return to a sequestered budget in fiscal year 2016, we will not be able to execute the Defense Strategy as it is conveyed in the 2014 Quadrennial Defense Review and a revision will be required.

CURRENT NAVY OPERATIONS AND READINESS

Employing a combination of Forward Deployed Naval Force ships homeported overseas and rotationally deploying units from CONUS, our Navy sustains a global presence of about 100 ships and submarines. Their combat power and other capabilities include the contributions of embarked Carrier Air Wings or other aviation units, Marine Expeditionary Units or elements of a Special Purpose Marine Air/ Ground Task Force, Coast Guard detachments, and Special Operations units, among others. These capabilities are further enhanced by land-based or expeditionary Navy forces in theater. With additional ships training in home waters, approximately half the battle force is underway or deployed on any given day.

Every hour of every day around the globe we are executing missions. The sun never sets on the U.S. Navy. Ballistic Missile Submarines sustain the most survivable leg of our nation's nuclear triad. Carrier Strike Groups (CSGs), Amphibious Ready Groups (ARGs) and attack submarines (SSNs) conduct named operations in support of the Combatant Commanders (COCOMs) or exercise with other nations to build the partnerships essential to the stability of the global system. Ballistic Missile Defense-capable Cruisers and Destroyers protect U.S. and allied sea and shore-based assets. Our units operate with other nations through exercises or through executing theater security cooperation plans; activities essential to the stability of the global system. As an example, last month, USS *Fort Worth* (LCS–3) practiced the Code for Unplanned Encounters at Sea (CUES) with the Chinese Navy, enhancing the professional maritime relationship between the U.S. Seventh Fleet and the People's Liberation Army-Navy [PLA(N)]. Our crews and platforms are trained and certified to execute their core capabilities across the spectrum of military operations and are ready to be re-tasked as required to meet the next challenge. This was the case in August 2014 when the *George HW Bush* CSG relocated from the Arabian Sea to the North Arabian Gulf and was on station, ready for combat operations, in less than 30 hours. The Navy is fundamentally multi-mission and rapidly adjusts to meet new challenges that might require U.S. presence and power projection forces.

Navy will continue to sustain the readiness of our deployed forces under our fiscal year 2016 budget submission, but it will require several years to fully recover the capability to rapidly respond to COCOM requirements for a major contingency. In addition to our forces that are globally deployed today, combined requirements include: three extra CSGs and three ARGs to deploy within 30 days to respond to a major crisis. However, on average, we have only been able to keep one CSG and one ARG in this readiness posture, 1/3 of the requirement. Assuming the best case of an on-time, sufficient, and stable budget with no major contingencies, we should be able to recover from accumulated backlogs by 2018 for CSGs and 2020 for ARGs—five plus years after the first round of sequestration.

Recovery of readiness also requires a commitment to protect the time required to properly maintain and modernize our capital-intensive force and to conduct full-spectrum training. Our updated force generation model—the Optimized Fleet Response Plan (OFRP)—is designed to meet this commitment as well as better align all elements that support readiness development. Achieving full readiness entails the restoration of required capacity to our public shipyards and aviation depots—primarily through hiring and workforce development. In addition to aviation depots backlogs, we must also overcome the challenges of extending the service life of our legacy F/A–18 Hornet aircraft to 10,000 hours. Underlying our plan is the need to operate the battle force at a sustainable level over the long term. With this plan we recover our material readiness, keep faith with our Sailors and their Families by providing more predictability in the operations schedule, and control the pace of deployments.

Meeting Our Readiness Challenges

The Navy fiscal year 2016 budget request continues to fully support the readiness of our deployed forces. The budget request sustains our credible and survivable sea-based strategic deterrent and with continued overseas contingency operations (OCO) funding meets the adjudicated requirements of the fiscal year 2016 Global Force Management Allocation Plan (GFMAP). This includes at least two CSGs and two ARGs, operating forward, fully mission-capable and certified for deployment. We continue to employ innovative approaches, including the use of new platforms like the Joint High Speed Vessel and the Mobile Landing Platform, to ensure the Navy/Marine Corps team continues to meet the security requirements of our nation, while providing the opportunity to reset and sustain the material condition of the force. Greater use of capable auxiliaries helps relieve pressure on our overstretched amphibious fleet.

Generating the Force

Navy readiness is at its lowest point in many years. Budget reductions forced cuts to afloat and ashore operations, generated ship and aircraft maintenance backlogs, and compelled us to extend unit deployments. Since 2013, many ships have been on deployment for 8–10 months or longer, exacting a cost on the resiliency of our people, sustainability of our equipment, and service life of our ships.

Navy has managed force generation using the Fleet Response Plan (FRP) since it was adopted in 2003 and fully implemented in 2007. This cyclic process was designed to support readiness by synchronizing periodic deep maintenance and modernization with the Fleet training required to achieve GFMAP forward presence objectives and provide contingency response capacity. However, the continued employment of our contingency response units to generate increased presence over the past decade has not only increased maintenance requirements, it has also limited their availability to complete required maintenance and training. As with previous testimony of the last few years, this practice is unsustainable.

In 2013 and 2014, for example, Naval forces provided six percent and five percent more forward presence, respectively, than allocated due to emergent operations and unanticipated contingencies. This unbudgeted employment amounted to greater than 2,200 days in theater over that approved on the global force management plan in 2013 and greater than 1,800 days in theater over in 2014. We should operate the Fleet at sustainable presence levels in order for the Navy to meet requirements, while still maintaining material readiness, giving ships time to modernize, and allowing them to reach their expected service lives.

This year, Navy began implementation of the Optimized Fleet Response Plan (OFRP) to address these challenges. Designed to stabilize maintenance schedules and provide sufficient time to maintain and train the force while continuing to meet operational commitments, OFRP aligns supporting processes and resources to improve overall readiness. Furthermore, it provides a more stable and predictable schedule for our Sailors and their Families. We will continue OFRP implementation across the FYDP.

Ship Operations

The baseline Ship Operations request for fiscal year 2016 provides an average of 45 underway steaming days per quarter for deployed ships and 20 days non-deployed, and would support the highest priority presence requirements of the Combatant Commanders to include global presence for two CSGs, two ARGs and an acceptable number of deployed submarines. With OCO, ship operations are funded at 58 steaming days deployed/24 days non-deployed. The requested funding will meet the full adjudicated fiscal year 2016 GFMAP ship presence requirement, support higher operational tempo for deployed forces and provide full operating funding for individual ship level maintenance and training.

Air Operations (Flying Hour Program)

The Flying Hour Program (FHP) funds operations, intermediate and unit-level maintenance, and training for ten Navy carrier air wings, three Marine Corps air wings, Fleet Air Support aircraft, training squadrons, Reserve forces and various enabling activities. The fiscal year 2016 baseline program provides funding to build required levels of readiness for deployment and sustain the readiness of units that are deployed. Navy and Marine Corps aviation forces are intended to achieve an average T–2.5/T–2.0 USN/USMC training readiness requirement with the exception of non-deployed F/A–18 (A–D) squadrons. Because of shortfalls in available aircraft due to depot throughput issues, these squadrons are funded at the maximum executable level while non-deployed, resulting in an overall readiness average of T–2.8/2.4. All squadrons deploy meeting theT–2.0 readiness requirement and OCO provides for additional deployed operating tempo above baseline funding.

Spares

The replenishment of existing, "off the shelf" spares used in ship and aircraft maintenance is funded through the Ship Operations and Flying Hour Programs. With OCO, those programs are fully funded in PB16. The provision of initial and outfitting spares for new platforms, systems and modifications is funded through the spares accounts. Traditionally, these accounts have been funded below the requirement due to limited funding or past execution issues. Due to the ultimate impact on readiness, PB16 sustains executable funding levels to reduce cross-decking and cannibalization of parts driven by large backlogs. This is complemented by Navy-wide efforts to improve execution of these accounts, which have shown considerable success in aviation spares over the last two years, and continues to be a focus area.

Readiness Investments Required to Sustain the Force—Ship and Aircraft Maintenance

The Navy maintenance budget requests are built upon proven sustainment models. They are focused on continuing our ongoing investment to improve material readiness of our surface combatants, and support the integration of new capabilities into naval aviation.

The fiscal year 2016 baseline budget request funds 80 percent of the ship maintenance requirement across the force, addressing both depot and intermediate level maintenance for carriers, submarines and surface ships. OCO funding provides the remaining 20 percent of the full baseline requirement to continue reduction of the backlog of life-cycle maintenance in our surface ships after years of high operational tempo and deferred maintenance. This year, the additional OCO for maintenance reset ($557M) includes funding for aircraft carriers (CVNs) as well to address increased wear and tear outside of the propulsion plant as a result of high operational demands. Since much of this work can only be accomplished in drydock, maintenance reset must continue across the FYDP.

To address the increased workload in our public shipyards and improve on-time delivery of ships and submarines back to the Fleet, the fiscal year 2016 budget grows the shipyard workforce, reaching a high of 33,500 personnel in fiscal year 2017, with additional investment in workforce training and development. One attack submarine (SSN) availability is moved to the private sector in fiscal year 2016 with plans for two additional SSN availabilities in the private sector in fiscal year 2017 to mitigate total workload. The fiscal year 2016 budget includes $89.5M in MILCON projects and $142M in restoration and modernization projects for Naval Shipyards in fiscal year 2016, for a total capital investment of 8.7 percent in these important facilities.

The Fleet Readiness Centers (FRCs), Navy's aviation depots, have been challenged to recover full productivity after hiring freezes, furlough, and overtime restrictions in fiscal year 2013. They face a growing workload, particularly for the additional service life extension of our legacy

F/A–18 Hornets. FRCs are aggressively hiring with a goal of reaching full capacity by the end of this year. The hiring of additional engineering support to address new repairs required to reach 10,000 hours of service life, reallocation of some of the workforce, and contracting for private sector support have all been undertaken to complete existing work-in-process at the FRCs, particularly for legacy Hornets. Field teams have been increased to improve flight line maintenance and understanding of the material condition of airframes coming to the depots. As new repairs and parts are identified and approved, kits are developed to ensure long-lead parts are readily available.

As a result of these challenges, the Aviation Depot Maintenance program is funded to an executable level of 77 percent in baseline, 83 percent with OCO for new work to be inducted in fiscal year 2016. This funding level supports a total of 564 airframes and 1,834 engines/engine modules to be repaired.

Navy Expeditionary Combat Forces

Navy expeditionary combat forces support ongoing combat operations and enduring Combatant Commander requirements by deploying maritime security, construction, explosive ordnance disposal, logistics and intelligence units to execute missions across the full spectrum of naval, joint and combined operations. In fiscal year 2016, baseline funding is improved significantly over prior years, providing 80 percent of the enduring requirement, with OCO supporting an additional 15 percent of the requirement.

Readiness Investments Required to Sustain the Force—Shore Infrastructure

The Navy's shore infrastructure, both in the United States and overseas, provides essential support to our Fleet. In addition to supporting operational and combat readiness, it is also a critical element in the quality of life and quality of work for our Sailors, Navy Civilians, and their Families. As we have done for several years, we continue to take risk in the long-term viability of our shore infrastructure to sustain Fleet readiness under the current funding level. However, in fiscal year 2016 our facilities sustainment is improved to 84 percent of the OSD Facilities Sustainment Model versus 70 percent this year. When restoring and modernizing our infrastructure, we intend to prioritize life/safety issues and efficiency improvements to existing infrastructure and focus on repairing only the key components of our mission critical facilities. Lessor critical projects will remain deferred. Overall, the Department of the Navy will exceed the mandated capital investment of 6 percent across all shipyards and depots described in 10 USC 2476 with a 7.4 percent total investment in fiscal year 2016. With the support provided by the Congress, Navy is on track to exceed the minimum investment in fiscal year 2015 as well.

Looking Ahead

As we look to the future, the Navy will continue to be globally deployed to provide a credible and survivable strategic deterrent and to support the mission requirements of the regional Combatant Commanders. Global operations continue to assume an increasingly maritime focus, and our Navy will sustain its forward presence, warfighting focus, and readiness preparations to continue operating *where* it matters, *when* it matters. We see no future reduction of these requirements and we have focused the fiscal year 2016 Navy budget submission to address the challenges to achieving the necessary readiness to execute our missions. Any funding below this submission requires a revision of America's defense strategy. Sequestration would outright damage the national security of this country.

In closing, we should recall that our Sailors are the most important element of the future readiness of the Navy. Fortunately, they are the highest quality, most diverse force in our history and continue to make us the finest Navy in the world. As the CNO says, "They are our asymmetric advantage." On behalf of all our Sailors (active and reserve), Civilians and their Families let me reiterate our appreciation for the continued support of the members of the committee.

Senator AYOTTE. Thank you, Admiral Howard.

I would like to now receive testimony from General Paxton, the Assistant Commandant of the United States Marine Corps.

Thank you, General Paxton.

STATEMENT OF GENERAL JOHN M. PAXTON, JR., USMC, ASSISTANT COMMANDANT, UNITED STATES MARINE CORPS

General PAXTON. Thank you, Chairman Ayotte, Ranking Member Kaine, Senator Rounds, and distinguished members of the Readiness Subcommittee. I appreciate the opportunity to appear before you today and to report on the readiness of your United States Marine Corps.

Today, as always, your Marine Corps is committed to remaining our Nation's ready force, a force that's truly capable of responding to a crisis anywhere around the globe at a moment's notice. I know that this committee and the American people have high expectations of your marines. You expect your marines to operate forward, to stay engaged with our partners, to deter potential adversaries, and to respond to crises. When we fight, you expect us to always win. You expect a lot of your marines. You should.

As we gather today, more than 31,000 marines are forward deployed and engaged, doing just what you expect and we expect them to be doing. Our role as the Nation's ready force continues to inform how we man, train, and equip the Marine Corps. It also prioritizes the allocation of resources which we receive from Congress. I can assure you that your forward-deployed marines are well trained, well led, and well equipped.

In fact, our readiness was proven last year, as your Marine Corps supported recent evacuations of United States citizens in South Sudan and then Libya and then Yemen. Those ready forces are also currently engaged in the Middle East, conducting strikes against Syria and Iraq, training Iraqi army units, and protecting our Embassy in Baghdad. They also routinely deploy and exercise across the Asia-Pacific region, where over 21,000 are west of the International Dateline.

These events demonstrate the reality and the necessity of maintaining a combat-ready force that's capable of handling today's crisis today. Such an investment is essential to maintaining our Nation's security and the prosperity for the future.

We will work hard with you in order to maintain the readiness of our forward-deployed forces. While we do that, we have not sufficiently invested in our home-station readiness and in our next-to-deploy forces. We have also underfunded or delayed the full funding for our modernization, for our infrastructure sustainment, and some of our quality-of-life programs. As a result, approximately half of our non-deployed units are suffering personnel, equipment, or training shortfalls. Ultimately, this has created an imbalance in our institutional readiness. At the foundation of our readiness, we emphasize that all marines and all marine units are physically and mentally ready, are fully equipped, and have sufficient time to train with quality small-unit leaders at the helm. They are, thus, ready to move out whenever they're called.

As we continue to face the possibility of full implementation of the Budget Control Act (BCA), our future capacity for crisis response, as well as our capacity for major contingency response, is likely to be significantly reduced. Quite simply, if our home-station units are not ready due to a lack of training, a lack of equipment or manning, it could mean a delayed response to resolve a contingency or to execute an operational plan, both of which would create unacceptable risk for our national defense strategy as well as risk to the limits of mission accomplishment or the physical risk to the force, itself.

The readiness challenge we already see today provide context for our messages this morning. Your United States Marine Corps can, indeed, meet the requirements of the defense strategic guidance with the President's Budget, but, unfortunately, there is no margin. As our chairman stated, even under PB–16, we are already at the ragged lower edge for readiness.

I thank each of you for your faithfulness to our Nation, for your support of the Department and all four of our services.

I request that my written testimony be accepted for the record.

I thank you for the opportunity to appear before you this afternoon, and I look forward to your questions.

Thank you.

[The prepared statement of General Paxton follows:]

PREPARED STATEMENT OF GENERAL JOHN PAXTON ASSISTANT COMMANDANT UNITED STATES MARINE CORPS

General Paxton was promoted to General and assumed the duties of Assistant Commandant of the Marine Corps on December 15, 2012. A native of Pennsylvania, he graduated from Cornell University with a Bachelor and Master of Science in Civil Engineering and was commissioned through Officer Candidate School in 1974.

General Paxton's assignments in the operating forces include Rifle and Weapons Platoon Commander and Company Executive Officer, Co. B, 1st Battalion, 3d Marines; Training Officer, 4th Marine Regiment; Executive Officer, Co. G, 2d Battalion, 4th Marines; Company Commander, Co. L and Operations Officer, 3d Battalion, 5th Marines; GCE Operations Officer, II MEF, and Assistant Chief of Staff, G–3, 1st Marine Division. He commanded the 1st Battalion, gth Marines in support of operations in Bosnia and Somalia and later the 1st Marine Regiment.

Other assignments include Company Commander, Co. B, Marine Barracks Washington and Commanding Officer of Marine Corps Recruiting Station New York. He served as a Plans Division Officer, Plans, Policies and Operations, HQMC; the Executive Assistant to the Undersecretary of the Navy; and Amphibious Operations Officer/Crisis Action Team Executive Officer, Combined Forces Command, Republic of Korea.

As a general officer, he has served as the Director, Programs Division,Programs and Resources, HQMC; the Commanding General of Marine Corps Recruit Depot San Diego/Western Recruiting Region; Commanding General,1st Marine Division; Chief of Staff, Multi-National Forces— Iraq; Director for Operations, J–3, The Joint Staff; and Commanding General, II Marine Expeditionary Force and Commander Marine Forces Africa. Most recently he served as the Commander, Marine Corps Forces Command; Commanding General, Fleet Marine Force Atlantic; and Commander, Marine Forces Europe.

General Paxton is a graduate of the U.S. Army Infantry Officer Advanced Course and Marine Corps Command and Staff College. He has also served as a Commandant's Fellow at the Brookings Institute as well as at the Council on Foreign Relations.

Introduction

Chairman Ayotte, Ranking Member Kaine, and distinguished members of the Senate Armed Services Subcommittee on Readiness: I appreciate the opportunity to testify on the current state of readiness in your Marine Corps and on our Fiscal Year 2016 budget request. We greatly appreciate the continued support of Congress and of this subcommittee in ensuring our ability to remain the Nation's ready force.

Since 1775 the Marine Corps, has been our nation's Crisis Response force. This was mandated by our 82nd Congress. Continuing to fulfill this role remains our top priority. Balanced air-ground-logistics forces that are forward-deployed, forward-engaged, and postured to shape events, manage instability, project influence, and immediately respond to crises around the globe are what we provide. Marine forces remain expeditionary and are partnered with the Navy, coming from the sea, operating ashore, and providing the time and decision space necessary for our National Command Authority. Ultimately, our role as America's 9–1–1 force informs how we man, train, and equip our force both for today and into the future.

This past year has demonstrated that the Marine Corps must be ready to respond, fight, and win more than just the last war. In 2014 the performance of your Marine Corps underscored the fact that responsiveness and versatility are in high demand today and that fact can be expected in the future.

YOUR MARINES—OPERATIONALLY RESPONSIVE

OEF—Afghanistan

In 2014, Marine Expeditionary Brigade-Afghanistan (MEB–A) concluded six years of sustained Marine Air-Ground Task Force (MAGTF) operations in Afghanistan. Operations there focused on ensuring the success of the Afghanistan presidential elections in the summer of 2014 and transitioning security responsibilities to the Afghanistan National Defense Security Forces (ANDSF). With Marines serving in an advisory capacity, the ANSF in Helmand Province held control of all district centers.

Regional Command (SW) also turned over operational responsibilities to the International Security Assistance Force Joint Command (IJC). Today, a residual Marine presence of several hundred continues to support the Resolute Support Mission (NATO)/OPERATION FREEDOM'S SENTINEL (US) in Afghanistan.

Special Purpose Marine Air Ground Task Force—Crisis Response (SPMAGTF–CR)
  Operations

While not as independent, flexible and responsive as our Marine Expeditionary Units (MEU) embarked and underway aboard Amphibious Ready Groups (ARG), two SPMAGTF–CRs are filling crisis response critical capability gaps for the combatant commanders in AFRICOM and CENTCOM. This past year SPMAGTF–CR units assigned to AFRICOM positioned forward in Moron, Spain and Signonella, Italy safeguarded the lives of our diplomatic personnel and conducted military-assisted departures from the U.S. Embassy in South Sudan in January and our Embassy in Libya in July 14.

The Marine Corps SPMAGTF–CR unit assigned to CENTCOM (SPMAGTF–CR–CC) became fully operational on 1 November 2014 and deployed to the CENTCOM AOR. Since that time, SPMAGTF–CR–CC conducted embassy reinforcement, Theater Security Cooperation (TSC) exercises, and provided critical aviation and ground capabilities in the fight against ISIL. Most recently, Marines from SPMAGTF–CR–CC supported the evacuation of our Embassy in Sana'a, Yemen in February of this year.

Current Operations

Today, there are over 31,000 Marines forward deployed, conducting a full range of theater security and crisis response missions. Marines are currently conducting security cooperation activities in 29 countries around the globe. Over 22,000 Marines are west of the international dateline in the Pacific building partnership capacity, strengthening alliances, deterring aggression, and preparing for any contingency. Your Marines serving today in the operating forces are either deployed, getting ready to deploy, or have recently returned from deployment. Our operational tempo since September 11, 2001 has been high and remains high today. We expect this trend to continue.

INSTITUTIONAL BALANCE

The Marine Corps is committed to remaining the Nation's ready force, a force truly capable of responding to a crisis anywhere around the globe at a moment's notice. Thus, the American people and this Congress have rightly come to expect the Marine Corps to do what must be done in "any clime and place" and under any conditions. As our 36th Commandant recently published in his Commandant's Planning Guidance (CPG), "you expect us to respond quickly and win always."

This obligation requires the Marine Corps to maintain a high state of combat readiness at all times. Readiness is the critical measure of our Marine Corps' capacity to respond with required capability and leadership. We look at readiness through the lens of our five institutional pillars of readiness—**high quality people, unit readiness, capacity to meet the combatant commanders' requirements, infrastructure sustainment, and equipment modernization**. These pillars represent the operational and foundational components of readiness across the Marine Corps. We know we are ready when leaders confirm that their units are well trained, well led at all levels, and can respond quickly to the unforeseen. This capability helps to minimize operational risk and provides our national leaders the time and space to make reasoned decisions.

While we will always ensure that our forward deployed Marines and Sailors are properly manned, trained, and equipped, we must seek a balanced investment across the pillars to simultaneously ensure current as well as future (i.e. next to deploy) readiness. At the foundation of this readiness, we emphasize that all Marines and all Marine units (i.e. from home station) are physically and mentally ready, are fully equipped, and have sufficient time with quality small unit leaders in place to move and train whenever called upon.

We also fully appreciate that our readiness and institutional balance today, and the ability to maintain it in the future, are directly related to today's fiscal realities. During these fiscally constrained times, we must remain focused on the allocation of resources to ensure the holistic readiness of the institution (i.e. training, education, infrastructure and modernization), making every dollar count when and where it is needed most.

As the Marine Corps looks to achieve balance across the five pillars of readiness after thirteen years of uninterrupted war, our efforts have been frustrated by two clearly tenuous variables. First, the continued high operational tempo of, and high demand for, Marine forces, and second, the continued budget uncertainty surrounding annual appropriations (i.e. sequestration and impacts). Both of these variables have been keenly and repeatedly felt throughout the Marine Corps all this year as we have protected near-term readiness at the expense of our long-term modernization and of our infrastructure investments. This reality has forced the Marine Corps' to make the hard choice to underfund, reduce or delay funding, which threatens our future readiness and responsiveness.

As America's 9–1–1 force, your Corps is required to maintain an institutional capability, an operational balance, and an expeditionary mindset that facilitates our ability to deploy ready forces tonight. However, as we continue to face the possibility of sequestration-level funding for FY 2016, we may well be forced into adopting some short term or limited scope and scale variations for future unexpected deployments over the next few years. This means quite simply, that we will see increased risk in timely response to crises, in properly training and equipping our Marines to respond, and in their overall readiness to respond. By responding later with less and being less trained we may eventually expect to see an increase in casualties.

Readiness and the Capacity to Respond

With the support of Congress, the Marine Corps is committed to remaining ready and continuing the tradition of innovation, adaptation, and winning our Nation's battles. The challenges of the future operating environment will demand that our Nation maintain a force-in-readiness that is capable of true global response. America's responsibility as a world leader requires an approach to the current and future strategic landscape that leverages the forward presence of our military forces in support of our diplomatic and economic elements of power.

As stated in the 2012 President's Defense Strategic Guidance, ''The United States will continue to lead global efforts with capable allies and partners to assure access to and use of the global commons, both by strengthening international norms of responsible behavior and by maintaining relevant and interoperable military capabilities.'' High-yield, relatively low-investment Marine Corps capabilities (ready and responsive air-ground-logistics forces) uniquely support this strategic approach.

CURRENT READINESS

Maintaining the readiness of our forward deployed forces during a period of high operational tempo while amidst fiscal uncertainty; as well as fiscal decline, comes with ever increasing operational and programmatic risk. Today, approximately half of the Marine Corps' home-station units are at an unacceptable level ofreadiness in their ability to execute wartime missions, respond to unexpected crises, and surge for major contingencies. Furthermore, the ability of non-deployed units to conduct full spectrum operations continues to degrade as home-station personnel and equipment are sourced to protect and project the readiness of deployed and next-to-deploy units. As the Nation's first responders, the Marine Corps' home-stationed units are expected to be at or near the same high state of readiness as our deployed units, since these non-deployed units will provide the capacity to respond with the capability required (leadership and training) in the event of unexpected crises and or major contingencies.

Despite this challenge and imbalance, the Marine Corps continues to provide units ready and responsive to meet core and assigned missions in support of all directed current operational, crisis, and contingency requirements. However, we continue to assume long-term risk particularly in supporting major contingencies in order to fund unit readiness in the near term. Consequently, the Marine Corps' future capacity for crisis response and major contingency response is likely to be significantly reduced. Quite simply, if those units are not ready due to a lack of training, equipment or manning, it could mean a delayed response to resolve a contingency or to execute an operational plan, both of which create unacceptable risk for our national defense strategy as well as risk to mission accomplishment and to the whole-of-force itself. The following sections elaborate on some specific readiness challenges the Corps is facing today.

CURRENT CHALLENGES TO READINESS AND THE CAPACITV TO RESPOND

As the Nation's first responders, we firmly believe that the Marine Corps as a service, and in its entirety, is expected to be always in a high state of readiness. Today however, there are numerous challenges that have created a readiness imbalance, affecting our capacity to respond to future challenges with the required capability and leadership. For example, our home station unit's ability to train is challenged. Time is the essential component required to fix worn equipment and to train units to standard. A lower end-strength and unwavering and high unit deployment to dwell (D2D) ratios exacerbate time at home stations to prepare, train, and maintain. This, coupled with temporary shortages of personnel and equipment at the unit level, validate operational requirements that exceed resource availability, and a growing paucity of amphibious platforms on which to train, all contribute to degraded full-spectrum capabilities across the entire Service. As an example, a D2D ratio of 1:2 means your Marines are deploying for 7 months and home for 14 months before deploying again. During that 14-month "dwell," units are affected by personnel changes and gaps (duty station rotations, schooling, and maintenance), ship availability shortfalls and growing maintenance requirements, equipment reset requirements (service life extensions and upgrades), degraded supply storages, training schedule challenges (older ranges and equipment, and weather) and more. These collective challenges factor into every unit's compressed and stressing task to remain constantly ready. In some case, the D2D ratio is even lower than 1:2 (MV–22 squadrons, Combat Engineer units, and F/A–18 squadrons), placing considerable stress on high demand, low density units and equipment. Also concerning is the inability to assess the long-term health of the force at lower D2D ratios and the impact on overall force retention. Quite simply, despite OIF and OEF being "over," the unstable world and "New Normal" is causing your Corps to continue to "run hot." As referenced earlier, just over half of Marine Corps home-stationed units are at unacceptable levels of readiness. For example, Marine Aviation contains some of our most stressed units. As operational commitments remain relatively steady, the overall number of Marine aircraft available for tasking and or training has decreased since 2003. At that time Marine Aviation contained 58 active component squadrons and 12 reserve component squadrons for a total of 70 squadrons.

The Marine Corps has 55 active component squadrons today, three of which (2 VMM, and 1VMFA) are in transition. Of the 52 remaining squadrons, 33 percent are deployed and 17 percent are in pre-deployment workups to deploy. Our minimum readiness goal to deploy is T–2.0, which is simply the cut line between a squadron trained to accomplish its core mission and a squadron that is not. To attain a T–2.0 rating, a squadron must be qualified to perform at least 70 percent of its Mission Essential Tasks (METs) (i.e. tasks required to accomplish the multiple missions that are or may be assigned to a unit). Currently, our deployed squadrons and detachments remain well trained and properly resourced, averaging T–2.17. Next-to-deploy units are often unable to achieve the minimum goal of T–2.0 until just prior to deployment. Non-deployed squadrons experience significant and unhealthy resource challenges, which manifest in training and readiness degradation, averaging T–2.96.

The Marine Corps is actively and deliberately applying resources to maintain the readiness of deployed and next-to-deploy units. Our focus is to continue to meet all current requirements, while addressing the personnel, equipment, and training challenges across the remainder of the force. We are in the midst of a comprehensive review of our manning and readiness reporting systems and will develop a detailed plan to enhance our overall readiness during 2015.

We are also committed to meet the growing expeditionary requirements of our combatant commanders (COCOMs). To meet COCOM requirements, the Marine Corps will be required to sustain a D2D ratio in the active component force of 1:2 vice a more stable, and time proven, D2D ratio of 1:3. The Marine Corps also has some high demand/low density units that maintain a current D2D ratio of less than 1:2, such as the (VMGR/KC–130) community. These communities are closely monitored for training, maintenance, and deployment readiness as well as deployment frequency. The Marine Corps will continue to provide ready forces to meet COCOM demands, but we are carefully assessing the impact of reduced D2D ratios on our training and quality of life across all units and occupational fields. What we do know is that the optimal size of your Marine Corps to meet the requirements of the Defense Strategic Guidance is 186,800 Marines. This optimal size gives the Marine Corps the capacity we need to meet current operational requirements demand with a D2D ratio closer to 1:3 which supports time for home station units to train and maintain. We continue to validate and support this assessment. Today, due to fiscal realities, the Marine Corps is adjusting its active duty end-strength to reach 182,000 Marines by 2017. As we continue to downsize, we must emphasize the enduring national mission requirement to provide forces that can always meet today's crisis response demands.

Another significant readiness challenge is the growing gap in the numbers of small unit leaders with the right grade, experience, technical skills and leadership qualifications associated with their billets. Specifically, our current inventory of Non-Commissioned Officers (NCOs) and Staff Non-Commissioned Officers (SNCOs) is not meeting our force structure requirements. The technical, tactical, and leadership demands on our NCOs and SNCOs has grown during 13 years of OIF and OEF. These Marine combat leaders have proven their mettle. We remain committed to fully and properly training them and their successors for the rigors of an unstable world with disaggregated operations against an asymmetric enemy in a distant and hostile environment. This dynamic directly affects our current and future training, maintenance, and discipline. We must train and retain adequate numbers of SNCOs and NCOs to preclude degraded crisis response readiness and ensure combat effectiveness. The Marine Corps' PB16 military budget funds a fiscal year 2016 end-strength of 184,000 in our base budget and supports right-sizing our NCO ranks to provide our Marines the small unit leadership they deserve and which our Corps and nation need.

NAVAL EXPEDITIONARY FORCE

We share a rich heritage and maintain a strong partnership with the United States Navy. Sea-based and forward deployed naval forces provide the day-to-day engagement, crisis response, and assured access for the joint force in a contingency. The availability of amphibious shipping is paramount to both our readiness and to our overall ability to respond. The Marine Corps' requirement for amphibious warships to respond, for war plans, and for contingencies remains at 38 platforms. The Navy's inventory today is 31 total amphibious warships. When accounting for steady-state demands and for essential maintenance requirements we are seeing that far fewer platforms are readily available for employment. Simply put we have a serious inventory problem and a growing availability challenge.

This is why the Marine Corps fully supports the Secretary of the Navy and Chief of Naval Operations' (CNO) efforts to increase the inventory and availability of amphibious platforms and surface connectors that facilitate our key concepts of operational maneuver from the sea (OMFTS) and ship-to-objective maneuver (STOM). The President's budget supports key investments in LPD–28, LX(R), and ship-to-shore connectors (SSC), and demonstrates our commitment to global maritime presence and to our Nation's mandate to sustain an amphibious capability that can respond to, deter, deny, and defeat threats on a global scale. We appreciate Congress providing a substantial portion of funding to procure a 12th LPD, and respectfully request that this committee continue to support full funding of that amphibious ship. The enhanced mission profiles of these new, improved and much needed platforms create operational flexibility, extended geographical reach, and surge capabilities for all our COCOMs.

Naval investments in alternative seabasing platforms expand access and reduce dependence on land bases, supporting national global strategic objectives and providing operational flexibility in an uncertain world. The naval seabasing investments in the Mobile Landing Platform (MLP), the Large Medium-Speed Roll-on/Roll-off (LMSR) strategic sealift ship, and the (T–AKE) Dry Cargo and Ammunition Ship as part of the Maritime Prepositioning Ship Squadrons (MPS), coupled with the Joint High Speed Vessel (JHSV), Afloat Forward Staging Base (AFSB) and ship-to-shore connectors provide additional lift, speed, and maneuver capability to augment, yet not necessarily replace or substitute for proven Navy and Marine Corps amphibious combat capabilities. Although never a substitute for amphibious warships, particularly in a contested environment, these alternative platforms will continually complement amphibious ships and can enhance national readiness and ability to answer COCOM non-combat demands.

While the President's Budget moves us in the right direction, it will take many years and a sustained effort to address the serious risk in the current inventory and availability of amphibious ships. The Marine Corps will continue to work closely with the Navy and Congress to implement the 30 year ship building plan and to address the current amphibious availability and readiness challenges.

Building the Force of the Future

As challenging as it has been to prepare Marines for the current fight, our force must adapt to the ever-changing character and conduct of warfare to remain ready, relevant, and responsive. Innovation and adaptability will be required to build the force of the future. For the last 14 years, the Marine Corps has applied a small but key percentage of our resources to providing Marines what tey need for today's fight. While individual Marines are our critical weapons system, we must outfit him with modem, reliable and useful gear and equipment. Because readiness remains our first priority in meeting our national security responsibility, our focus on an unrelenting demand for forces coupled with a declining budget has forced the Marine Corps to make difficult choices and to reduce investment in modernization in order to maintain current and near term readiness. We are consciously, by necessity, delaying needed modernization.

MODERNIZATION EFFORTS

Our declining budget has forced the Marine Corps to make difficult choices at the expense of modernization to maintain current and near term readiness. In the current fiscal environment, the Marine Corps is investing only in essential modernization, focusing on those areas that underpin our core competencies. Today, we have placed much emphasis on new or replacement programs such as our Amphibious Combat Vehicle (ACV), a Joint Light Tactical Vehicle (JLTV), our CH–53K Heavy Lift Replacement, and the critical fifth generation F–35 Joint Strike Fighter (JSF). At the same time, our modernization resources are also necessarily focused on improving capabilities and extending the life of current systems in order to fill gaps that can be exploited by today's threats.

In order to balance modernization across the capabilities of the MAGTF and ensure a ready and responsive force of the future, our two top priorities remain the ACV, to include science and technology efforts toward high-water speed capabilities, and the JSF, both of which provide the technology required to dominate our adversaries in the future. Additionally, our investments in Network On-the-Move (NOTM), Ground/Air Task Oriented Radar (G/ATOR), and other additional aviation platforms such as the MV–22, CH–53K, and UH–1Y/AH–1 Z programs are vital to the overall combat effectiveness and readiness of our future MAGTFs. We are also focused on and investing heavily in extending the service life and improving the interim capabilities of our legacy systems due to the time required to recapitalize needed capabilities while ensuring a smooth transition to future requirements.

For example, the need for recapitalization of our 42-year old AAV is critical and the nation cannot afford to gap this capability. Rising annual maintenance costs for the AAV and other legacy systems compete for resources against modernization efforts that seek to replace them with modern combat capabilities (i.e. ACV). This required allocation of precious resources works against our other investment and recapitalization efforts. Additionally, for our legacy aircraft platforms, the focus is on modernization to make them relevant in tomorrow's fight while simultaneously providing a bridge to rearrange our aviation recapitalization efforts. Rapid procurement of these new systems is critical to solving both our serious current and future readiness problems.

If we do not modernize, we will actually move backwards. Our adversaries continue to develop new capabilities exploiting any technology gaps associated with specific domains and functions. By under-resourcing equipment modernization we will ultimately fall behind. Increasing threats, the proliferation of A2/AD weapon systems, and the aging of key material capabilities present an unacceptable risk to forcible entry operations and our overall combat effectiveness if modernization continues to be diminished or halted.

Modernization and innovation are more than just procurement programs. We will re-energize our MAGTF experimentation and test new tactics, techniques, procedures, equipment and concepts that will allow us to meet every challenge. We are maintaining our commitment to Science and Technology, and we continue to look for opportunities to expand our efforts in this critical area.

CONCEPT DEVELOPMENT AND EXPERIMENTATION

The current and future operating environment will remain volatile, unpredictable, and complex. To continue to deliver order from the chaos, we anticipate no lessening in the demand for Marine capabilities ranging from Amphibious Ready Groups with enhanced Marine Expeditionary Units (ARG/MEUs) and Special Purpose MAGTFs for crisis response as well as for more Marine Security Guards at our embassies and consulates (MCESG). Trends point to greater security challenges to our vital national interests almost everywhere. Therefore, as our Nation meets these future challenges, it will rely heavily on the Marine Corps to remain the ready, relevant, and responsive force of first resort. While there will be a degree of consistency in our missions, there is likely to be inconsistency in the operating environment, and we must be willing to experiment, take risk, and implement change to overcome challenges in those varied operating environments (threat, access, communications, etc.). As was the case prior to World War II, the quality and focus of our concept development, our expansion of science and technology, the :frequency and significance of our exercises, and our constant experimentation efforts will remain critical to our overall readiness, relevance, and indeed our mission success. The end state of our efforts to link concepts and doctrine to exercises and experimentation will be to develop and nurture the intellectual energy and creativity of individual Marines and of units. This will enable the Marine Corps to continue to be a leader in both tactical and operational innovation.

A year ago we published *Expeditionary Force 21 (EF–21)*, our Marine Corps capstone concept. *EF–21* establishes our vision and goals for the next 10 years and provides guidance for the design and development of the future force that will fight and win in the future environment. *Expeditionary Force 21* will also inform decisions regarding how we will adjust our organizational structure to exploit the value of regionally focused forces and provide the basis for future Navy and Marine Corps capability development to meet the challenges of the 21st Century. Developed in close coordination with the recent update of our maritime strategy (i.e. *Cooperative Strategy 21 (CS21))*, *Expeditionary Force 21* describes how the Marine Corps will be postured, organized, trained, and equipped to fulfill the responsibilities and missions required around the world. This comprises four essential lines of effort: refining our organization, adjusting our forward posture, increasing our naval integration, and enhancing littoral maneuver capability.

ALL VOLUNTEER FORCE

Our Marines and civilians are the foundation of who we are and of all that we do. We succeed because of our focus on recruiting, training, and retaining quality people. People are the primary means through which the Marine Corps remains ready and responsive in guaranteeing the defense of our great Nation. The resources we dedicate to recruiting, retaining, and developing high quality people directly contribute to the success of our institution. Thus, our commitment to attract, train, and deploy with the best quality Marines must always remain at the forefront.

Today, the Marine Corps does not have the proper level of personnel stability or cohesion in our non-deployed units. Having to move Marines between units to meet manning goals for approaching often accelerated or extended deployment cycles creates personnel turbulence, inhibits cohesion, and is not visible in our current readiness assessment tools. This personnel turbulence affects our combat readiness and our ability to optimally train, retain, and take care of Marines. Moving forward, we will improve cohesion by increasing our individual and unit preparedness across the force as well as emphasizing consistency of leadership and personnel stability across that same force.

Conclusion

On behalf of the Marines and Sailors and their families, all of whom provide this Nation with its versatile and reliable force-in readiness, I thank Congress and this subcommittee for your continued interest in and recognition of our operational and fiscal challenges and our key contributions to national security. We are proud of our reputation for frugality and remaining one of the best values for the defense dollar. In these times of budget austerity, the Nation continues to hold high expectations of her Marine Corps, and our stewardship of taxpayer dollars. The Marine Corps will continue to answer the Nation's call to arms, meet the needs of the Combatant Commanders and others who depend upon our service, and operate forward as a strategically mobile force optimized for forward-presence and crisis response. Your continued support is requested to provide a balance across all five of our readiness pillars, so we can maintain our institutional readiness and our ability to remain responsive . . . as your predecessors wisely charged more than 60 years ago, "to be the most ready when the nation is least ready."

Senator AYOTTE. Thank you, General Paxton.

We'll now receive testimony from General Spencer, who is the Vice Chief of Staff for the United States Air Force.

Thank you, General Spencer.

STATEMENT OF GENERAL LARRY O. SPENCER, USAF, VICE CHIEF OF STAFF, UNITED STATES AIR FORCE

General SPENCER. Thank you, Madam Chair, Ranking Member Kaine, and Senator Rounds, and distinguished members of the subcommittee. Thank you for your continued support of America's airmen and their families, and for the opportunity to share the Air Force's current readiness posture.

The United States Air Force is the most globally engaged air force on the planet, and our airmen are defending the Nation through a wide spectrum of activities, from dropping bombs and flying space assets to delivering humanitarian relief and protecting the homeland. We remain the best air force in the world. But, recent budget cuts, coupled with 24 years of combat operations, has taken its toll.

Our airmen, your airmen, have always been, and will always be, the cornerstone of the Air Force. Combatant commanders tell us that our airmen continue to perform exceptionally well across the globe. However, we are the smallest and oldest air force we have ever been, while demand for air power continues to grow. This is not a complaint. We're happy that what we bring to the table is recognized as indispensable when it comes to meeting the Nation's objectives. But, I am concerned. In fact, I'm more concerned than I—today than I was when I testified last year.

We have tankers that are, on average, 52 years old; bombers that are over 50 years old; and fourth-generation fighters that are, on average, 25 years old. In 1991, if we had used the B–17 bomber to strike targets in Baghdad during the first Gulf War, it would have been younger than the B–52, the KC–135, and the U–2 are today. We have to modernize to maintain our technological advantage, and this is something that we've set aside, the last few years. Our potential adversaries have been watching us and now know what it takes to create the best air force in the world. They are investing in technologies and doing everything they can to reduce our current airpower advantage.

Because we have the smallest and oldest air force in history, we need all of our airmen to be proficient in every aspect of their mission. Unfortunately, our high operations tempo has caused our airmen to only be proficient in the jobs they perform when they deploy. We simply do not have the time and the resources to train airmen across the full range of Air Force missions. I'm confident that, with your help, we can reverse this trend and regain our readiness. But, we will have to make some difficult choices to balance capacity, capability, and readiness, all of which have already been cut to the bone.

Our fiscal year 2016 President's Budget submission aims to balance critical operational training and modernization commitments, but, even at this level, it will take years to recover lost readiness. We have already delayed major modernization efforts, cut manpower, and reduced training dollars.

One final point. The capability gap that separates us from other air forces is narrowing. That gap will close even faster under BCA levels of funding. When sequestration first hit in 2013, we saw the domino effect it had on our pilots, maintainers, weapons loaders, air traffic controllers, and our fighters and bomber squadrons. Readiness levels of those central to combat operations plummeted. In short, we were not fully ready. We cannot afford to let that happen again.

To quote a young C–17 instructor pilot, ''I am committed to defending this Nation anytime and anyplace, but I need the training and equipment to be ready to perform at my best.'' This is critical to answering the Nation's call to fly, fight, and win.

I'd like to thank you all for the opportunity to be here today, and for your continued support of your Air Force. I'm now happy to take your questions.

Thank you.

[The prepared statement of General Spencer follows:]

PREPARED STATEMENT OF GENERAL LARRY O. SPENCER, VICE CHIEF OF STAFF OF THE AIR FORCE

Introduction

The United States Air Force has never failed to meet any threat our Nation has faced and establish an environment that was beyond the capabilities of our enemies to resist. Our capabilities of range, speed, and agility give our Nation an indispensable and qualitative advantage that is unparalleled today and we must retain them going into the future. Whether it's opening an aerial port to deliver humanitarian aid, flying a single sortie from middle-America to the Korea peninsula and back to send a clear message, dropping a bomb, or dropping a Brigade Combat Team into the conflict zone—we can reach out and touch anyone, anytime, at any place, in a matter of hours, not days. Since 1947, Americans have been able to sleep soundly knowing that in every corner of the globe, the United States Air Force is ready.

Through technology, ingenuity, and unparalleled training and expertise the Air Force provides our Nation and allies more precise and effective options. But readiness requires the right number of Airmen, with the right equipment, trained to the right level, and with the right amount of support and resources, to accomplish what the Nation asks us to do. While Airmen have performed exceptionally well in major combat operations such as those in Iraq, and Afghanistan, these operations come at a price. Today, continual demand for airpower, coupled with dwindling and uncertain budgets, leave the force with insufficient time and resources to train Airmen across the full range of Air Force missions. Proficiency required for highly contested, non-permissive environments has suffered, due to our necessary engagement in the current counterinsurgency fights.

We recognize that there are no quick fixes. Even at the level of the President's Budget it will take the Air Force years to recover lost readiness. Our return to full-spectrum readiness must include the funding of critical programs such as flying hours, weapons system sustainment, and infrastructure, while also balancing deployment tempo, training, and exercises. We must also be technologically superior and agile enough to evolve ahead of the myriad of future potential threats.

However, because of the current restrictive and uncertain fiscal environment we have been forced to make difficult choices within an incredibly complex security environment. Our current Service readiness and capacity are degraded to the point where our core capabilities are at risk. To correct this, the fiscal year 2016 President's Budget (FY16 PB) preserves the minimum capability to sustain current warfighting efforts, and places the Air Force on a path toward balancing readiness with necessary modernization in order to meet evolving threats.

Readiness Today; Readiness Tomorrow

The 2012 Defense Strategic Guidance (as updated by the 2014 Quadrennial Defense Review) requires healthy and sustainable Air Force combat readiness, modernization and recapitalization programs. Since passage of the Budget Control Act, the Air Force has been forced to trade capacity in an attempt to preserve capability. We are now at the point where any further reduction in size equals a reduction in capability—the two are inextricably linked. Combatant commanders require Air Force support on a 24/7 basis, and the Air Force does not have excess capacity to trade away. If asked to accomplish multiple parts of the defense strategy, we will have to make difficult decisions on mission priorities and dilute coverage across the board. Unless we improve readiness levels, our full combat power will take longer to apply, will pull coverage from other areas, and will increase risk to our Joint and coalition forces.

The FY16 PB is a step to alleviate some of that risk. It allows us to preserve our future readiness, including munitions inventories; protect our top three acquisitions programs; and protect investments such as the training aircraft system, cyber mission forces and the next generation of space systems. Our plan is to reduce risk in high-priority areas by accelerating the modernization of aging fleets and improving our installations around the country. We are focused on capabilities, not platforms—preserving and enhancing the agility and flexibility of the Air Force.

Weapons System Sustainment

Weapons system sustainment (WSS) is a key component of full-spectrum readiness. Years of combat demands have taken a toll across many weapons systems. We continue to see an increase in the costs of WSS requirements. These costs are driven by factors such as the complexity of new systems, operations tempo, force structure changes, and growth in required depot-level maintenance on legacy aircraft.

If sequestration-level funding returns, it will hamper our efforts to improve WSS. Depot delays will result in the grounding of some aircraft. It will mean idle production shops, a degradation of workforce proficiency and productivity, and corresponding future volatility and operational costs. Analysis shows it can take up to three years to recover full restoration of depot workforce productivity and proficiency. Historically, WSS funding requirements for combat-ready forces increase at a rate double that of inflation planning factors. WSS costs still outpace inflationary growth, and in the current fiscal environment, our efforts to restore weapons systems to required levels will be a major challenge.

The longer we fly our legacy aircraft, the more they will break and require increased preventative maintenance. We have tankers that are on average 52 years old, bombers that are over 50 years old, and fourth generation fighters that are an average of 25 years old. If we had kept WWII's B–17 bomber, and flown it in Operation Desert Storm 1991, it would have been younger than the B–52, the KC–135, and the U–2 are today. If we are not able to perform weapons system sustainment on our aircraft or modernize them so we can improve upon their speed, range, and survivability, we will lose our technological edge and superiority.

Flying Hours and Training

Our flying hour program is essential to full-spectrum readiness. If sequestration is implemented, it will affect our ability to accomplish flying and training requirements and our ability to meet full-spectrum operations. Readiness is not just influenced by funding, but also ongoing operations. Time and resources used to conduct current operations limit opportunities to train across the full-spectrum of missions. For example, the operational and combat demands over the last decade have eroded our ability to train for missions involving anti-access/area denial scenarios. To meet combatant commander requirements, we have had to increase our deployment lengths and decrease time between deployments, which affect our reconstitution and training cycles. Our high operations tempo has resulted in Airmen that are only proficient in the jobs they do when they deploy.

To fix this problem and be able to meet an increasing demand for Air Force capabilities in future operations, we need the funding and the latitude to balance these rotational and expeditionary requirements with adequate full-spectrum training. The additional funding requested in the FY16 PB will help us recover flying hour-related readiness due to the fiscal year 2013 sequester and put us on a steady path toward full recovery.

Operational Training Infrastructure (OTI)

Full-spectrum training for combat against a high-end adversary requires specific investment and emphasis on an integrated training and exercise capability. This includes the availability and sustainability of air-to-air and air-to-ground training ranges, fully augmented by, and integrated with, virtual training in simulators and with constructive models to represent a high-end adversary. This is what we call our Operational Training Infrastructure (OTI). Our ability to effectively expose our forces to a realistic, sufficiently dense, and advanced threat capability cannot be accomplished without our focus on OTI.

OTI becomes critical when you consider that we must expand our 5th generation weapon systems. These systems are so advanced that challenging our operators in live training environments while protecting the capabilities and tactics of these systems is problematic. Our approach to OTI will address these training shortfalls while maximizing the value of every training dollar.

In addition to investments in simulators as part of OTI, our ranges are used for large-scale joint and coalition exercises that are critical to training in realistic scenarios. We intend to sustain these critical national assets to elevate flying training effectiveness for the joint team and improve unit readiness. The same is true for our munitions. The FY16 PB includes funding to addresses the shortfalls in our critical munitions programs and to accelerate production and reduce unit cost.

Space Readiness

Space-based capabilities and effects are vital to US warfighting and the Air Force remains committed to maintaining the advantages this domain provides. Potential adversaries are developing and fielding capabilities to deny us these advantages and are also fielding their own space capabilities to support their terrestrial warfighting operations. We now recognize that space can no longer be considered a sanctuary. In order to deter and defeat interference and attacks on US space systems we must improve space domain mission assurance capabilities against aggressive and comprehensive space control programs.

Nuclear Readiness

The FY16 PB strengthens the nuclear enterprise, the number one mission priority of the Air Force. The Air Force's intercontinental ballistic missiles and heavy bombers provide two legs of the Nation's nuclear triad. The FY16 PB funds additional investments across the FYDP to sustain and modernize the ICBM force and funds 1,120 additional military and civilian billets across the nuclear enterprise as part of the Secretary of the Air Force-directed Force Improvement Program.

CONCLUSION

A ready, strong, and agile Air Force is a critical component of the best, most credible military in the world. Air Force capabilities are indispensable to deterrence, controlled escalation, and destruction of an adversary's military capability ... as well as development, stability, and partnership-building. Today's Air Force provides America an indispensable hedge against the challenges of a dangerous and uncertain future, providing viable foreign policy options without requiring a large military commitment on foreign soil.

Such a force does not happen by accident; it must be deliberately planned and consistently funded in order to be successful. Continued investments in Air Force capabilities and readiness are essential to ensuring that the Air Force maintains the range, speed, and agility the Nation expects. Regardless of the future security environment, the Air Force must retain—and maintain—its unique ability to provide America with *Global Vigilance*, *Global Reach*, and *Global Power*.

Senator AYOTTE. Thank you, General Spencer.

In light of the fact that we've had President Ghani here, I wanted to, in particular, ask General Allyn and General Paxton about what is happening on the ground in Afghanistan. In—you know, in particular, I was pleased to hear the President's announcement this week that he has decided to leave 9,800 troops in Afghanistan until the end of the year. However, it seems to me that, as we look forward, having spoken to General Campbell and others about the situation in Afghanistan, that, even after this year, the most prudent course forward would be a ground—a conditions-based determination of what we do with those 9,800 troops. So, could you speak to that issue for me, in terms of where we are in Afghanistan and the needs we will have, going forward? You know, and I think one of the things all of us took from the President's speech today is, we actually have a partner that we can work with. That is refreshing.

So, General Allyn?

General ALLYN. Thank you, Madam Chair.

I was fortunate to be in Afghanistan with General Campbell the first week of February, and I had an opportunity to deploy down to be with both of our divisions that are forward, providing mission command—one from Kandahar, at Regional Command South, Tactical Air Command South (TAC–South), and the other one in TAC–East, from the 3rd Infantry Division stationed at Bagram. What was very clear to me as they were posturing for the potential to have to draw down to the directed numbers by the end of the year was that we had increased the ratio of our soldiers to contractors to a level that was what I would call the ''razor's edge of risk.'' We had contractors doing that which soldiers need to do to assure the security of our forces. It was really driven by the force manning levels that General Campbell was posturing for to accomplish the mission.

I also had an opportunity to meet with two of the senior commanders from the Afghan Security Forces that I had served with in 2011 to 2012 in Regional Command East, and I asked for their assessment of where they thought the Afghan Security Forces were and what gave them concern. They were, overall, very optimistic, very determined, and very confident that they could weather the battle against the Taliban if they had the critical enabling capability that they required from—you know, from the United States—and, in specific, some of the—closing the gap for them, in terms of their aviation and their close air support capability that is not yet fully developed, and to continue to mature their sustainment capacity. Both efforts are well underway by the joint team that is there on the ground in Bagram under General Campbell's leadership. I concur with you that the ground that we have been able to regain with the partnership between General Campbell and President Ghani is very, very inspiring, certainly to us, who have not had that experience in the last couple of years, but it's also very inspiring to the Afghan Security Forces. Because President Ghani has personally gone down to spend time with his forces and communicate his intent to enable them to fight and win. So, I think it bodes well as we look forward, ma'am.

General PAXTON. Yeah, thank you, Madam Chair. I, too, have had the opportunity on many occasions to be over in Afghanistan and, just several months ago, with our Marine Expeditionary Brigade (MEB) Alpha, who was down in Helmand Province before they pulled out. I'd echo what General Allyn said a moment ago, in that the conditions for success in Afghanistan have been set, both at the tactical level as well as at the strategic level. Making events on the ground and the commitment to continue there be more conditions-based than time-based is always a good thing. I feel good for General Campbell and our national leadership that, by making things condition-based, we have set ourselves on a path for success over there, and set the government as well as the Afghan National Security Force on the conditions for success.

President Ghani committed as much to the Department of Defense and the Armed Forces when he was over at the Pentagon the other day. So, I think we're in a good trajectory now, ma'am.

Senator AYOTTE. Thank you both.

I wanted to follow up with General Spencer and Admiral Howard on the issue of—we're engaged with, obviously, still the mission against ISIS, which has involved significant use of our fighters that, if we had met probably a year ago, we wouldn't have been talking about some of the additional use of our fighter force in regard to this fight that we face and challenge that we face there. Can you help update the—both of you update me on where—what are our challenges, in terms of having enough fighters, given that this is sort of a situation that we're, on the air, really helping the Kurds and the Iraqis on the ground fight the fight? You know, where do you see that, in terms of extra push on the force? As we do the authorization, what would you like us to think about that, just in terms of the current situation on the ground in Iraq and Syria?

Admiral HOWARD. Thank you, Senator.

So, as I mentioned in my opening statement, as we maintain carriers about—the *George Herbert Walker Bush* was there, and first the fighter size started to fly nontraditional Intelligence, Surveillance and Reconnaissance (ISR), but then quickly went into strike missions. As we stay committed in these endeavors, we will most likely maintain carrier presence over there. What we're finding is, we're flying the aircraft at a higher operational tempo. So, as we move forward and we continue staying engaged in support to the land components, we end up flying these aircraft much longer, longer distances, and then we end up consuming their readiness. We're seeing that play out as we try and extend the life of these fighters, particularly the legacy Hornets, from 6,000 hours to 10,000 hours.

Then, as we go through and we do maintenance on them, we're finding that the additional flight time has created deterioration problems that we just weren't expecting. So, as Senator Kaine pointed out, it would have been this morning's testimony, the more—the higher the OPTEMPO and the more we're engaged, the more we're flying, and then the more hours we put on these aircraft, and then the longer it is to return them back to a flyable status. So, we're clearly committed to the—any—the support that we're tasked to provide, but it does consume readiness.

Senator AYOTTE. General Spencer?

General SPENCER. Yes. Madam Chair, first of all, I echo everything that Admiral Howard had—Admiral Howard said. I'd like to—but, let me add a couple of things to give you some context.

Back during Desert Storm, in the Air Force, we had 133 combat aircraft squadrons—133. We—during Desert Storm, we deployed 33 forward, so we had a lot of squadrons left to do something else if something came up in the world. Today, we have 54 fighter squadrons—54 total. So, I would ask you to think back, if we were in Desert Storm today and we deployed 33 forward. So, that's problem number one.

The other issue is—and that we've—I assume we'll get into, here—is readiness, because a lot of folks assume you deploy folks to war and they are as ready as they can get. But, that's not the case in a counter insurgency (COIN) fight, because they're getting a lot of training, flying and dropping smart munitions, but they don't have the sophisticated surface-to-air threat that they would have in a more—in a higher-level fight. So, part of our challenge is, we are continually deploying folks to the current war. We don't keep them back home long enough to go out and train on these higher-level threats.

The final challenge I would mention is, we are using up a lot of smart munitions, and—which are expensive—and the interesting thing about the OCO budget is, overseas contingency operations (OCO) allows us to replace smart munitions that have already been expended. It doesn't let us project ahead.

Senator AYOTTE. Really?

General SPENCER. So, we—we're always chasing ourselves, getting behind in the amount of munitions we have.

So, to add a couple with Admiral Howard's comments, I couldn't agree with you more.

Senator AYOTTE. Thank you.

I'd like to turn it over to Senator Kaine.

Senator KAINE. Thank you, Madam Chair.

Thanks, to the witnesses, for your testimony.

General Allyn, you said something—I tried to write it down fast, and I'm having a hard time reading my handwriting, during your testimony, but I think it was, "We have enough readiness for immediate consumption, but not enough for a contingency.'' Is that basically the thought you were expressing?

General ALLYN. Yes, it is, Senator Kaine. We—for the past, you know, in—about 6 months after sequestration, our readiness had degraded to about 10 percent of our brigades being ready for a global contingency. The next 18 months, we rebuilt that to just above 30 percent. But, we have been holding steady at 30 percent now for about 4 months, because, as fast as we generate the readiness, it's being consumed.

As an example, when the ebola crisis hit—

Senator KAINE. Yeah.

General ALLYN.—you know, within days, we deployed the 101st Airborne Division, that was a force training and ready to go to Afghanistan, to divert in and provide essential support to the U.S. Agency for International Development (USAID) to fight and abate the Ebola crisis. We also deployed a Brigade Combat Team of the 82nd Airborne Division into Iraq to provide the plus-up and advise-and-assist capability that was required in Iraq. Their readiness was, you know, absolutely at the top, because they had just handed off the Global Response Force mission to the 2nd Brigade of the 82nd. We had sort of counted on that brigade coming off to provide some surge capacity for a number of months, but, instead, you know, a requirement emerged, and we met it, just as we always will.

So, as we've been, you know, being good stewards of the resources you are giving us to generate readiness, we are also responding to emergent requirements.

Senator KAINE. Right.

General ALLYN. In 2014, about 87 percent of the emergent requirements, we met as an Army, as we will continue to do, but it does speak to the—really, the twofold challenge of building readiness. You know, we can generate additional readiness, but we can't control the demand.

Senator KAINE. Right. Right. Is that just basic, kind of, phraseology, ''We have readiness for immediate consumption, but not for a contingency''? Would that be kind of a fair statement that all of you from your respective branches would agree with?

Admiral HOWARD. So, in particular for the Navy, we look at the readiness of the units that we deploy and then the forward-deployed units, and then we've always kept a level of readiness for the units in order to surge, those that respond to a contingency, just as General Allyn described. Right now we're at our lowest surge capacity that we've been at in years, and—so, we're able to have two carriers out and about, but we've only got one in backup. The same with the amphibious ready group (ARG). We've got two out and about and one in backup.

Our goal is to—with this budget, to get us back and increase that readiness and meet our own goals of two—having two carriers deployed and three ready to surge, approximately half the force.

So, yes, as time has gone on, we have literally consumed the readiness, and then the readiness of the forces that are next in the wicket.

Senator KAINE. Great, thank you.

General Paxton?

General PAXTON. Thank you, Senator Kaine.

I guess the short answer is, absolutely, we generate readiness, but we consume it as fast as we generate it. We, as a Corps, are focused primarily on crisis response. As we do that, we are mortgaging our future for sustainment and for modernization, and we're also reducing the at-home or home-station training and availability of units.

I can give you two examples, if I may, Senator. One is in the Africa Command (AFRICOM) area, and one is in the Central Command area. In both of those geographic combatant commanders today, we have a Special Purpose Marine Air-Ground Task Force. We would like to say that is kind of like a MEU, a Marine Expeditionary Unit. It is not as sustainable and expeditionary ashore, and it certainly doesn't have the power projection and sovereign capability that we would like to have coming off of an amphibious platform, a ship. But, we generated those two capabilities in immediate response to combatant commander requests. In the case of AFRICOM, it was to help with some security-force arrangements at some embassies, to work some train, advise, and assist missions and develop partnership capacity. Then, in the Central Command area of responsibility (AOR), it was because of specific risks at two embassies, and then also to start working on train, advise, and assist missions with the Iraqi Security Forces.

But, in both of those cases, that has now consumed what would have been home-station readiness, because it's now forward deployed. It has brought us closer to a one-to-two depth-to-dwell, which creates stress on the force. It further exacerbates the age and the maintenance of our equipment. Despite the good work of my shipmate and where the Navy's trying to go with capital investment, it highlights the fact that we already have a paucity of amphibious ships by inventory, and that's also exacerbated by the fact that they have maintenance challenges keeping them in the yard. So, we can't generate enough sovereign launch-and-recovery capability for the Nation that we have to do these things with a smaller unit and go what we call "feet dry" ashore. So, we consume it as soon as we generate it, yes, sir.

Senator KAINE. General Spencer?

General SPENCER. Yes, sir. The—first of all, a similar story from—for the Air Force. The combat air forces that we have right now, less than 50 percent are fully spectrum ready—less than 50 percent. Let me give you a couple of examples, because, again, we're—right now we're just talking about combat air forces. We haven't talked about nuclear, we haven't talked about ISR, we haven't talked about space. But, let's talk about ISR for a second.

I mean, right now we have been in a position of surge in our ISR caps since 2007. That does not define a surge. So, we are essentially—

Senator KAINE. Because nobody ever asks for less ISR.

General SPENCER. That's exactly right.

Senator KAINE. It just continue—it continues to—

General SPENCER. It continues—

Senator KAINE. Yeah.

General SPENCER.—it has exploded—the demand has exploded. So, we have been staffed, if you will, for 55 cap since 2007, flying

65. We've—we surged, that entire time. So, we have essentially at our wits' end at the—where we are now, because we've got—remotely piloted aircraft (RPA) pilots are that we have just worked to the point where we are worried that we—whether we can retain them, or not, and whether they will stay.

Now—so, when we first started ISR, as you know, we did a combination of things. We brought in pilots from other airplanes, other weapon systems, brought them in, taught them how to fly RPAs, and we also created a schoolhouse to train new RPA pilots.

We've now reached the point where the new RPA pilots are coming up to the point where they can separate. We have asked them all, in a survey, ''Are you going to take the bonus and stay?'' Roughly 30 percent say they'll stay. We've already reached a point where our pilots can go back and fly other weapon systems, and we're telling them they can't go back. So, we're asking for volunteers to come back in, we're increasing their bonuses. We're asking for Guard, you know, to volunteer. We're—we have a series of things we're doing to try to make that enterprise healthier, but it's just an indication of what the current Ops Tempo has done. I can't—I want to footstop that, because General Paxton mentioned it. The Ops Tempo that we're under now has now allowed us to bring the—where we are down low enough so we can—

Senator KAINE. Yeah.

General SPENCER.—train and get ready to go again.

Senator KAINE. Right. Well, I'm over time, but just to say, you know, if we have, essentially, a force that's ready for immediate consumption, but we don't really have the contingency ability, you've just got to look at the world and say, ''So, are we in a world without contingencies, or are we in a world that is likely to throw some contingencies?'' The answer to that is just as plain as everyday's front page. We are in a contingency-rich world right now.

So, thank you, Madam Chair.

Senator AYOTTE. Senator Rounds.

Senator ROUNDS. Thank you, Madam Chair.

Thank you for your service.

Admiral Howard, a week ago today we had a group of South Dakotans in for a meet-and-greet. One of the guys was about my age, brought in and was very proud of the fact that in his wallet he was carrying a picture that his son had taken at his first solo flight in an F/A–18. In doing so, we could see the pride. But, he said something that was concerning to me, and that was that it was just unfortunate that it was taking approximately 18 months for them to reach a certain level of readiness, where, if they would have had the parts to keep the aircraft in the air, it would have taken normally about 12 months. It seems to me that, if that anecdotal information being shared is accurate, that you're going to have a tough time coming up with the pilots, in a regular order of operation, just to replace and keep up with the readiness necessary for the folks that are working right now in combat areas.

Could you visit a little bit about—number one, is my estimate—or is my information accurate, in terms of the challenges you've got right now with keeping aircraft in the air and operational? Second of all, with OCO funding the way that it's set up right now—and

I'm going to ask this of all of the members here—is there something that we can do, with regards to the limitations that we've got, to where we can modify OCO somehow so that you can access funds that might otherwise be there, but not available for what your immediate needs are?

Admiral HOWARD. Thank you, Senator.

Perhaps a slightly different perspective. This gets down to that 2013, when we sequestered, we furloughed some of our artisans and engineers, and then we created a backlog in our aviation depots. So, when we're looking at the throughput of those aviation depots, coupled with the aging aircraft, and then as we open up those older F/A–18s and discover that, by flying them longer, there's more corrosion, that backlog just increased. So, we already had the—have and are living with the impact of that short period of sequester. We now are in the timeframe where we are hiring the artisans as quickly as we can, several hundred this year, to help get us to being able to assess those aircraft quickly and then repair them as quickly as we can.

This is where OCO has been very helpful. So, we have our fundamental aviation maintenance account, and then we've plussed-up that maintenance account to help get that throughput up to where it needs to be, and to decrease that backlog.

So, for us, right now the limitations for the depot is not the money. The limitation is literally getting the people hired and in place; for the people who are new, getting them trained. But, there's also another piece to it. I think there's a trust factor there, that, when we want to bring people—proud civilians in to do all the support for our aircraft, or whether it's ships, they have to trust that the work's going to be there, that they can live their lives, pay their mortgages, and not worry about being furloughed, so that they want to have a job with the government.

So, we know we have a backlog, and we expect to be able to clear that up in 18 months. But, all bets will be off if we sequester again. Then, you're right, then it gets down to, not just, ''Do we have the aircraft for our pilots to train in?''—but, when we sequestered last time, I was the Deputy Commander of Fleet, and I had the very unhappy job of going down and talking to a cruiser community officer (CO) and his chiefs and his crew, because we weren't going to be able to get that ship underway. We talked about what it meant for their qualifications, what it meant for the—their ability to serve at sea. If people can't do their jobs, it's an immense dissatisfier.

Thank you.

General ALLYN. Senator Rounds, in terms of the OCO flexibility that's required, clearly OCO has been critical for us to meet the readiness and the equipment recovery, replenishment for our forces that have been deployed in support of the countless operational requirements, both emerging and known. We've been thankful for that funding. But, as you talk about a wider application of OCO in the future, it needs to be more flexible. It must be more flexible. Because, otherwise, we cannot use it for all the readiness requirements that we have, and certainly the year-to-year application of it—

Senator ROUNDS. Sir, if I could, would you get us a list of what you need the flexibility on that we may be able to look at, in terms of OCO funding available?

General ALLYN. Yes, sir, we will.

[The information referred to follows:]

General ALLYN. The Army, like each of the other services, needs the fiscal flexibility to address the uncertainty of funding we are dealing with, in a world were instability is creating increased overseas requirements. What we really need is sufficient base funding, but where feasible, we need broader discretion on the use of already appropriated Overseas Contingency Operations (OCO) funds in order to maintain the readiness of our formations and to respond to new missions. An example is what has occurred in Europe due to the Russian annexation of Crimea. This created a demand for the Army to defer sending an active component Brigade Combat Team to Kosovo, and instead, we sent it to Eastern Europe to deter and assure. To backfill that brigade, which was responding to a named operation, we mobilized a National Guard unit to go to Kosovo. Current OCO rules do not allow us to use OCO to pay the mobilization costs of the National Guard unit, instead we used base funding and had to reduce the readiness of other units to pay for those costs. Allowing for more flexible use of OCO, for direct and indirect impacts to named operations that may not occur in the geographic area of the named operation, would greatly improve our readiness.

Admiral HOWARD. I have nothing further to add to my response.

General SPENCER. Senator Rounds' question was directed to General Allyn, not General Spencer.

General PAXTON. The largest issue concerning flexibility in OCO funding is timing. The Marine Corps begins to plan its requirements for the OCO budget approximately 18 months before the funding would likely be made available. Even with our best forecasting, requirements will change during the year of execution, requiring transfers between accounts, many of which require Congressional approval.

Additionally, the planning process for long-term modernization, sustainment and upgrade programs requires a lengthy, multi-year timeline. Since the OCO budget is developed outside the normal Planning, Programming, Budgeting and Execution process, it is difficult to use on critical shortfall procurement items in the current year.

Senator ROUNDS. Thank you.

General PAXTON. Yeah, thank you, Senator Rounds.

If I may, two things. Number one, to follow up on Vice Chief of Naval Operations' (CNO) comments, when we have a challenge with our maintenance and the dollars for maintenance—and you used F–18s as an example. We call it RBA, Ready Basic Aircraft. Those are the ones that are through the upgrades, modernization, and they're ready on the flight line to take off. When those aircraft are delayed, either because we don't have money for parts, money for engineers, or money to actually move the aircraft to the depot, we still have pilots who are waiting to fly. So, now we have more pilots than we have aircraft. Sometimes, if we have a higher demand signal, those pilots may actually go forward. So, the time they have available to train to them when they get back is shorter. So, you can see the downward spiral that happens, because then you have more pilots with a shorter-term time, with less aircraft to train on, and then you get in this training readiness spiral that goes down.

If you exacerbate that by the fact that some of those flight requirements actually have to come from the deck of the ship that you need bounces on carrier calls or that you need night vision goggle ops, the minute you perturb the availability of a ship or an aircraft, the spiral starts, and it's really hard to regain.

To your second question, on OCO dollars, always helpful. We'll all work together to get you examples of how that would help. But,

I'd just like to be on the record, sir, that the OCO dollars are insufficient to the problem we have right now. I mean, they are single-year dollars. It's a short planning horizon. It's actually the BCA caps and it's the ability to forecast across the Future Years Defense Program (FYDP) to start long-term modernization programs and sustainment and upgrade programs that will eventually allow us to not only handle the crisis, but to handle the contingency we need because we have enough readiness at home station.

Thank you, sir.

General SPENCER. Senator, in terms of OCO specifically, flexibilities of where you may—might be able to help, I already mentioned one. So, there are certain things, like munitions, that are after-the-fact. So, we put, in our OCO submission, munitions that we used last year, but we can't put in OCO submission what we plan to use this year. So, again, we're always a year behind.

Timing is really critical, because if the OCO budget comes late in the year, that does a lot of things to us. One, we are trying to plan, hoping on the come, not exactly sure what we'll get passed. There is actually a law that says you have to obligate 80 percent of our own end money by July. So, if the money comes late, we've got a problem there that we have to work through.

We're all afraid to death one of these days, if OCO goes away, and a lot of the things that are being funded in OCO, quite frankly, will end up in our base. How is that going to work? You know, in the Air Force, for example, we have several bases in the theater right now that we've been told are going to be, quote/unquote, "enduring," which means we'll probably hang onto those bases. They're being funded by OCO. What happens when OCO goes away? How do we get that money into the base?

Finally, as General Paxton mentioned, planning is a really big deal, because—particularly in a procurement account. So, if we're going to buy a weapon system, if we're going to pay for F–35s or do a multiyear for C–130s, it—that's really difficult to do if you're trying to do that one year at a time, because you don't know what's going to come in the next few years. So, to the extent that those type of purchases can—you know, I've been told that there's a—there is—that we have had a multiyear OCO in the past, or a supplemental. I don't know if that's under consideration. But, the real answer for us is if we can get that money in the base, that would really be helpful.

Senator ROUNDS. Thank you, Madam Chair.

Senator AYOTTE. Thank you.

It would be really helpful to us, especially those of us that serve jointly on the Budget and Armed Services Committee, if all of you could submit to us what you think, in terms of flexibility for OCO, because we don't know how this story ends, this year, and just—you know, you're, I'm sure, aware of things that happen on the floor on the budget and all that. It would be helpful for us to understand that. If the plus-up ends up being in the OCO line versus the base budget, what do you really need, to do what needs to be done? I know it's not ideal. Frankly, there are many of us that want to deal with the overall BCA in solving it. I'm still committed to doing that. But, you know, we've got to do what we've got to do around here. So, just—if you can get that to us, it would be helpful—all of the branches—to understand what you really need.

[The information referred to follows:]

General ALLYN. Receiving OCO funding instead of base funding for fiscal year 2016 would allow the Army to conduct its missions and achieve readiness targets provided that appropriation language and OMB interpretation fully allowed OCO dollars to be spent on base requirements. However, in the long term, using OCO to circumvent Budget Control Act caps would put Army readiness at risk, because steady, predictable base funding is the key to long term, enduring readiness.

Admiral HOWARD. What we really need is what we have included in the fiscal year 2016 Navy budget submission. As we look to the future, the Navy will continue to be globally deployed to provide a credible and survivable strategic deterrent and to support the mission requirements of the regional Combatant Commanders. Global operations continue to assume an increasingly maritime focus, and our Navy will sustain its forward presence, warfighting focus, and readiness preparations. We see no future reduction to these requirements. The fiscal year 2016 Navy budget submission addresses the challenges to achieving the necessary readiness to execute our missions.

Overseas Contingency Operations funding is meant to fund incremental costs of overseas conflicts such as in Afghanistan and Iraq. OCO does not provide a stable, multi-year budget horizon. Our defense industry partners need stability and long term plans—not short-term fixes—to be efficient and cutting-edge. OCO is dispiriting to our force. Our personnel, active, reserve and civilian and their families deserve to know their future more than just one year at a time.

The Navy appreciates Congress' continued action to explore alternative paths that do not lock in sequestration. Any funding below our Navy budget submission requires a revision of America's defense strategy. Sequestration would outright damage the national security of this country.

General SPENCER. *Question.* It would be really helpful to us, especially those of us that serve jointly on the Budget and Armed Services Committee, if all of you could submit to us what you think, in terms of flexibility for OCO, because we don't know how this story ends, this year, and just—you know, you're, I'm sure, aware of things that happen on the floor on the budget and all that. It would be helpful for us to understand that. If the plus-up ends up being in the OCO line versus the base budget, what do you really need, to do what needs to be done? I know it's not ideal. Frankly, there are many of us that want to deal with the overall BCA in solving it. I'm still committed to doing that. But, you know, we've got to do what we've got to do around here. So, just—if you can get that to us, it would be helpful—all of the branches—to understand what you really need.

Answer. The fiscal year 2016 President's Budget supports our critical needs to execute the defense strategy, but we made tough choices in capacity and capability / modernization. The Air Force does not support any reductions to the President's Budget and the short term solution of using OCO does not address the long term budgeting challenges created by the Budget Control Act (BCA). Further, this short term solution does not provide the necessary BCA relief for the other Federal Agencies that the Air Force works with such as Homeland Security and Department of Energy. Without relief for the other Federal Agencies, our partner missions will be at risk. Most importantly, this solution does not move us towards a more stable budget environment that is critical to long term strategic planning to meet the Defense Strategic Guidance and protect the Homeland.

General PAXTON. The largest issue concerning flexibility in OCO funding is timing. The Marine Corps begins to plan its requirements for the OCO budget approximately 18 months before the funding would likely be made available. Even with our best forecasting, requirements will change during the year of execution, requiring transfers between accounts, many of which require Congressional approval.

Additionally, the planning process for long-term modernization, sustainment and upgrade programs requires a lengthy, multi-year timeline. Since the OCO budget is developed outside the normal Planning, Programming, Budgeting and Execution process, it is difficult to use on critical shortfall procurement items in the current year.

Senator AYOTTE. I wanted to ask, General Allyn, can you give us an update on end strength and where we are, in terms of numbers, on end strength? How many people have we had to use involuntary terminations for in 2014? What's been the status of those individuals? You know, are they—are there people that we have in combat that we're giving involuntary terminations to? Then, you know, one thing I think that's fairly powerful as we look at—if we go to sequester, where does that put our end strength? I know we've talked about it in the larger committee. But, also, what does that mean, in terms of involuntary terminations?

I really want people to understand. I think this committee understands very well. In some ways, when we talk about sequester, when you talk to the Armed Services Committee, a little bit like preaching to the choir, but we want to get this word out also to the broader Senate. So, if you could comment on the involuntary termination issue, end-strength numbers. I would also then ask General Paxton to follow up the same with the Marine Corps.

General ALLYN. Yes, Madam Chair. The bottom line is, we are at about 498,000 today in the United States Army, headed toward a end-of-fiscal-year number of 490,000 and budgeted in the, Program Objective Memorandum (POM) to go down to 450,000. To give you the broader answer first, to get to 450,000 soldiers, as has been directed by our current budget, that will require the involuntary separation of 14,000 soldiers. On average—that's officers and noncommissioned officers—on average, it's about 2,000 per year. Okay? So, fiscal year 2014 was about 2,100 soldiers. Just over 50 percent of those soldiers served over two or more combat tours. So, these are soldiers that answered the call multiple times to meet the requirements that the Nation had. They were—

Senator AYOTTE. Two or more combat tours.

General ALLYN. Two or more combat tours for 50 percent of that—those that we were asking to leave involuntarily. Now, first and foremost, this is not a choice the United States Army took. This is a budget-driven requirement. So—

Senator AYOTTE. I assume that, if you've done two tours, you're not terminating these people because they aren't capable of fighting.

General ALLYN. You are absolutely accurate. You asked a question, were we really having to separate some soldiers that were forward deployed? The answer is yes.

Let me first let you understand that treating those veterans of multiple combat tours with dignity and respect is our absolute number-one commitment. Every single officer or noncommissioned officer that we asked to involuntarily separate was briefed, before the board was held, by a general officer—first general officer in the chain of command, and then, when the board completed its process and identified those for separation, they were briefed again, face to face, as much as possible. In a couple of cases, they had to have the general officer contact by phone or video teleconference (VTC) with the immediate commander present to ensure that we treated these, you know, people who had served so courageously with the absolute utmost dignity and respect.

Our objective in notifying people that were forward deployed was to give them the maximum time possible to transition effectively to the next phase of their life. The minimum that we wanted to provide them was 10 months, at least, so that they would have an opportunity to take the benefit of all of the transition, education, plug them into employment advisors through programs like our Soldier for Life Initiative, and ensure that we set them up for success, to include providing opportunities for mentors from industries around their communities that they intend to go back to.

So, not a choice that we took willingly or voluntarily, but we have taken it on, we have ensured the appropriate care of every one of our soldiers, and are committed to do so as we go forward.

Senator AYOTTE. General Paxton?

General PAXTON. Yeah, thank you, Senator Ayotte.

Your Marine Corps today is 184,000. We had grown to 202,000 by some special appropriations and authorizations. That was temporary. We knew we were not going to be able to sustain that. So, we had started our downward growth, if you will, before BCA kicked in.

Under BCA, we have to be at 182,000 by the end of fiscal year 2017. We expect, if full BCA continues, we could very well have to go to 175,000.

To date, we have deliberately not broken faith with marines. Almost all of our separations have been voluntary. We have had low double digits of majors who were not selected to lieutenant colonel, and staff sergeants who were not selected to gunnery sergeant, who we did not continue. But, they were afforded other venues for separation at that time.

We do have a concern that if the BCA caps come back and we have to go to 175,000, that at some point we could be forced to do larger numbers of involuntary termination.

Senator AYOTTE. I don't know if—you know, Admiral Howard, I'm not trying to exclude the Navy and the Air Force on this. Anything you want to report on this end?

General SPENCER. I would only add that we've—we were on a steady decline in manpower, and finally have—we've drawn a red line at around 317,000 for active duty, because we just can't go any lower. Based on our—the levels of maintenance folks we have on our flight lines, fixing our airplanes, launching satellites, we've sort drawn a red line and said we can't go any further.

Admiral HOWARD. So, along with General Spencer, I think the Navy and Air Force were on a different journey these last 15 years. I recall, in December of 2000, when I reported to the Joint Staff and then 9/11 happened the following year, literally I—we were a Navy of about 14 carriers, 383,000 people, and I think it was close to 312 ships. We're—we've downsized about 67,000 people, and we're about 279 ships today

The budget we've submitted continues to acquire ships, build ships, and we would be looking at being back to 304 ships in 2020. But, because we're a capital-intensive force, our manning is matched to those ships. So, we would expect to be at 329,000, and about 57,000 Reserve. But, we took—we reduced our force over the last 14 years. So, along with the Air Force, we're not trying to get any smaller.

Senator AYOTTE. Thank you.

Senator Kaine?

Senator KAINE. On the issue of OCO and flexibility, I'm maybe a little bit like a former Governor. We're all into flexibility. I like giving folks flexibility.

But, I would guess that, as long as we're talking about readiness, even putting flexibility doesn't necessarily—I think, General, you said, it's the caps, not the flexibility. Flexibility would be helpful. But, won't there always be a tendency, if you have to choose between priorities, to kind of short readiness? I mean, you're always going to—you're always going to do the day's mission and try to have people as well deployed as you can for doing a deployed mission. If you don't have enough to choose from, you'll always pick that, and probably try to save on the readiness side. It seems like that's one of the challenges. So, even if you allow for flexibility, it would seem that readiness is always going to be somewhat at risk in a capped environment when there aren't sufficient resources, "Well, we can't—we don't want to short the folks who are forward deployed during these missions, so we'll probably—you know, if we have to save it somewhere, we're going to save on the readiness side."

So, flexibility, I don't view that as the real solution. I mean, it could be helpful, but it's not really going to solve the readiness challenge we have, in my view. Am I wrong to look at it that way?

General PAXTON. Senator, if I may, I'll start, only because we've just had this discussion this morning in the building. Although there are some common terminologies and lexicon, each of the services has to look—

Senator KAINE. Yeah.

General PAXTON.—at this in a little different way.

So, on the part of the Marine Corps, we truly envision ourselves as the 9–1–1 force that you—that the American public, the American Congress, the taxpayer, they expect us to be most ready when everybody else is least ready. We don't have a big role or mission in the nuclear triad and things like that. We're a rather conventional force, we're a rather small-unit force, and we're supposed to be forward deployed, forward engaged. So, we fully expect that we're going to generate readiness and consume readiness, and, at some point, we will take risk in some modernization and we'll take risk in some home-station readiness. We think we're at that ragged edge right now.

For example, our aircraft are old, too, anywhere from 22 to 29 years, and growing. Our amphibious vehicle capability is 42 years old. So, we're at the point, as General Spencer said earlier, that we have to modernize. We, early on, after Operation Iraqi Freedom (OIF) and Operation Enduring Freedom (OEF), went into this bathtub, and we had to go all in to modernize, because the gear was too old.

So, we feel at risk now for modernization and sustainment. But, we're going to continue to give you fight-tonight forces, ready forces for the crisis that's at hand, even if we know, later on, we may eventually get to the point of, "Yes, but," that we'll give you several companies, but not a whole battalion, we'll give you a squadron with 8 aircraft instead of 12 aircraft.

But, each of the other services, at some point, looks at it just a little differently. So, that's where the Marine Corps is, sir.

General SPENCER. Yes, Senator. You put your finger on really what our challenge is, quite frankly, because you said, in most cases, we would go to readiness if we had a budget issue, a budget concern. The reason we do that is because we don't have a lot of choice. We've only got three pots of money. We have people, procurement, and readiness. People, you can't just send people home. I mean, you know, you—even if—people—actually, our military folks were exempt from sequestration, but, even if they weren't, that's a long process to reduce. Quite frankly, we can't reduce any more. Similarly with procurement, those are multiyear purchases that are stretched out over many years, involve a lot of money. If you start cutting those, your unit cost goes up.

Senator KAINE. Yeah, you can slow down the next one, but you can't—

General SPENCER. That's—

Senator KAINE.—break the one that you're—

General SPENCER. That's exactly right.

Senator KAINE.—in the middle of. Right.

General SPENCER. So, then—so, a lot of times, we don't have any choice, if we have to find fast money, but to go to readiness, because it's essentially Operations and Maintenance (O&M) money. But, that's the dilemma, because we—that's where our readiness is. So, that's the box we're put in.

Senator KAINE. Yeah.

General SPENCER. We don't want to do that. We're—all the services are obviously a little bit different, but, at least in the Air Force's case, as you know, you know, if we get called upon, I mean, we've got to be there in hours, not days, weeks, or months. So, it's—we have to—readiness is critical for us, yet readiness is the only account we can go reach out and take money quickly. So, that's the sort of dichotomy we're in.

Senator KAINE. Indeed.

Other comments? General Allyn, Admiral Howard?

General ALLYN. I was just going to just reinforce my teammates' points, here. But, it really does come down to trying to balance concurrent priorities. As has been stated, the Army's budget, over 50 percent of it is committed to our national treasure, our people, you know, both the military and civilian. So, we've got 50 percent of the budget with which we wrestle with the dual priorities of readiness and modernization. We, in the Army, have actually erred on the side of delivering the readiness that's required for the known and emerging missions, and taking risk in the mid- to long-term with modernization. But, that is a—that's a hard choice, and it's a choice that our Chief and our Secretary take, fully analyzing, you know, the opportunity costs of doing that.

It's just a very, very difficult position to be in, and one—with the capacity that this Nation has, we shouldn't be in that position.

Senator KAINE. Yeah.

General ALLYN. You know, our soldiers should expect that, when they go up against an adversary, that adversary faces an unfair fight whenever they come up against the United States of America. We are putting that at risk.

Senator KAINE. Admiral Howard?

Admiral HOWARD. Senator, thank you. I just wanted to share that, when I was at fleet, when we sequestered last time, as General Spencer pointed out, that was the only intermediate choices we had.

Senator KAINE. Yeah.

Admiral HOWARD. When you talk about readiness, we had to cancel deployments of ships. Now you're not where you need to be, and you're not giving the COCOM any forces, let alone ready forces.

Then we had to reduce steaming hours and flying hours, which is the training of the piece Senator Rounds brought up. We had to take some of the air wings down to tactical hard deck to generate the savings to hit that lower target budget—budget target. So, there is, in the immediate aftermath of sequestration, an impact on the forces and—in the Operations and Maintenance (O&M) account and in operations and in training dollars.

Thank you.

Senator KAINE. Last—just a comment. You had—you mentioned the COCOM, and that reminded me of one other thought. We have the hearings with the COCOMs, you know, the status hearings, during the spring. One of the things I'm really always impressed by, and most recently a conversation with General Kelly at SOUTHCOM, is the degree to which the COCOMs really approach their mission with kind of a whole-of-government approach. They're relying on the intelligence community, they're relying on the State Department, they're relying on Department of Justice, they're relying on the Department of Homeland Security (DHS)—especially in the SOUTHCOM, that's really important. All these agencies are affected by sequester, too, the partners that our COCOMs rely on. They may not be—you know, it may not be defense sequester, but they're sequestered on the nondefense side, and they have a direct impact on the security mission. So, again, there's a lot of compounding effects here, and your testimony is good tribute to that.

Thank you, Madam Chair.

Senator AYOTTE. Senator Rounds.

Senator ROUNDS. Thank you, Madam Chair.

I think it's becoming obvious in the discussion that, as you listen to us, we talk about trying to make it—we're trying to set it up so that there is a way to skin this cat that's out there right now with BCA basically there and in front of us. Part of it is to give you as many options as possible in order to be able to utilize the funds that we are able to allocate, either through the budget and then through the appropriations process. I want to make sure that, if we do take a particular approach, that it is as readily available to you as possible without other strings attached to it. So, you know, we're not exactly sure how we skin this cat that's in front of us, but we want your help in doing so, and that's the reason for the discussion.

I just wanted to go directly to General Spencer with something that you said earlier that I think is just so impactful, and that is that, if we would have been going to war in 1991, we would have been in the same position as we are today with the age of our aircraft; we'd be flying B–17s. You know, in fact, if my information is correct, the Department of Defense (DOD) currently operates a bomber force that is half the size of the Cold War force recommended by its 1993 bottom-up review.

Now, if it's true that advances in sensor technologies and precision-guided weapons have helped to offset cuts driven by budget reductions, but—in other words, they have the effect, though, of act-ing as a force multiplier—but, that being said, reduced readiness levels—and that's what we've been talking about here, are the readiness levels—the readiness levels have an opposite effect.

I'd just like to talk a little bit, and I want to give you an opportunity to visit a little bit, about the—what happens with the—has the combination of reduced readiness and smaller force size eroded our global strike advantage? Right now we're talking about aircraft that are very, very old, and you've got an F–35 that's available right now that you're still trying to procure, you've got a tanker that's necessary to be set up and operational, but you also have a need to replace, or at least to supplement, the B–1 and the B–2. Right now you've got B–52s that are doing some of that work, but the Long Range Strike Bomber (LRSB) has clearly got to be maintained, as well, or at least you've got to be able to procure that in the future. Can you talk a little bit about what that is and what's going on right now within the Air Force to try to maintain all of those goals, and procure and still maintain readiness?

General SPENCER. No, thank you, Senator.

Again, you've put your finger right on the issues, here. You know, the—we've only got 20 B–2s, and if—so, if we have to have a long-range penetrating bomber that can get through a lot of the—you know, back when the B–52 and the B–1 was built, they aren't stealthy, they don't—they won't penetrate some of the systems that are out there now, so we have to have that capability. Similarly, for our other platforms, as well. The F–35, for example, along with the F–22, you know, some of—there are other fighters being introduced into the market now, so-called 4.5 generation, if you will, that would beat our—I mean, the advantage that we have always had, and I think we still have, is, our pilots are better trained. But, if you give the adversary a better airplane, then that's a real problem.

So, the faster and the more efficiently we can get to fifth generation, the better.

Senator ROUNDS. Do you want to talk just a little bit in—you made the remark, and then you moved on rather quickly, but you're talking about a 4.5, which is out there, which is going to, basically, be in a position to where—we don't ever want to be in a fair fight, but we want to the advantage to be on our side all the time. Do you want to talk about that just a little bit?

General SPENCER. Sure, yes. So, the—they are being produced, as we speak, developed and produced, a fighter that is ahead of our fourth-generation—the F–15, F–16s—it is ahead. So, based on the systems they have, we—they would—as our Chief said, 4.5 kills a fourth-generation airplane. So, that's why it's—and the sense of—we have to modernize our fleet, is what I'm saying. The age of our fleet that we have now won't—is not sufficient for us in the high-end threats and the high-end fights that we are—that we could be involved in. So, we—so, if nothing else, to maintain, first, deterrence, but then to be able to win if deterrence fails. We want to go in—as General Allyn said, we don't want a fair fight. We want the best equipment, with the best technology, with the best-trained both—maintenance folks, pilots, you name it, space operators—we need the absolute best that we can have. So, that's really imperative for us to stay on track with our modernization.

Senator ROUNDS. Thank you, Madam Chair.

Unless one of the other—

Sir?

General PAXTON. Thank you, Senator Rounds.

If I may—I had made the point earlier about how we all need a planning horizon. We had aging aircraft in both our F–18s, our AV–8Bs and our EA–6s. We knew we were going to have to replace them, so we put—we went all in on the F–35, and we're in that bathtub right now. So, the monies and the planning that is available to us to bring the F–35 to fruition are critical for the fight in the future. If we don't—if the BCA kicks in and we buy fewer, then you lose the economies of scale, you delay the production line, and then our fight-tonight force and our fight-tomorrow force are both jeopardized.

Thank you.

Senator ROUNDS. Thank you.

General ALLYN. I would just add, for the Army, the same application that General Paxton just talked about for our—modernization of our aviation fleet is absolutely the exact same dynamic. So, we will not procure the more modern UH–60 aircraft that our total force needs, we will not modernize the AH–64 to the level that it needs to, and our CH–47 modernization will stop after fiscal year '16. So, it is absolutely critical that we stay on this path.

Admiral HOWARD. So, we have often used a technological edge as a warfighting edge. So, as we've had to meet budget targets, we've had to slow modernization down. But, really what that gets to is our ability to win in a anti-access aerial-denial fight. So, as we slow down our ability to modernize weapon systems on ships or on aircraft or the physical platforms themselves, it's given potential adversaries an opportunity to get closer to us and to start—and that gap in the technological edge is starting to diminish.

Senator ROUNDS. Thank you.

Thank you, Madam Chair.

Senator AYOTTE. So, I wanted to—we have—Senator Shaheen is on her way for some questions—but when—Admiral Howard, when we met in my office, one of the issues that you raised, we saw, recently, the attempt by ISIS to expose our men and women in uniform in the cyber domain. So, I wanted to get your thoughts on, you know, What are the cyber challenges that our forces face, and how does all this relate to readiness and our posture?

Admiral Howard, I'd start with you.

Admiral HOWARD. Thank you. So, there's two issues. All of us—one is the force, writ large—our civilians, our Active, and our Reserve. We all actually live and operate in this domain. We're in it for our workday, and then, for our sailors and Reserve, they're in it when they're off duty. So, for us, we have to continue to develop and train our workforce to understand that as much innovation and excitement and fun as you can have on liberty in this domain, there's vulnerabilities in this domain. Because of the robustness of knowledge exchange in this domain, the vulnerabilities translate to potential operational security issues, which is some of what we saw this week.

So, as—whether they're sailors, Reserves, or civilian, if they are out and about on social networks, and identify themselves or identify units, that they have to be trained to understand operational security in this virtual domain, just as they understand operational security in the physical domain.

The next piece is, there is a more professional cohort when you look at the—for us, the information dominance community, you look at our enlisted, our IT, and then, for officer, informational professionals, cryptologists, intelligence officers, and then they are really the heart of our cyber warriors and the workforce that we're developing to not only defend our networks, but also develop both offensive cyber capability, as well. Then, that's—for us, those are the components, those are the folks we put together, and then they are the ones that work underneath U.S. Cyber Command in whatever mission sets they're required to provide.

General ALLYN. Madam Chair, I would just add that, you know, in 2013, we had no Army cyber mission teams. Today we have 24 that are supporting combatant commanders at the initial operating capability, building to over 40, you know, by the end of next year. Their training and development is absolutely critical.

But, you highlighted a very critical point, and that is, we should be trying to accelerate the elimination of our vulnerabilities. Unfortunately, all of us are faced with the reality of having to take a multiyear approach to this, because of funding limitations. My belief is, this cyber risk is accelerating very, very fast.

General PAXTON. Senator, if I may, the—it also shows—to General Allyn's point, it shows the dynamic here—I'm sorry—it shows the dynamic of the pressure we're under. As the money gets tighter—BCA cap, if you will—and as the pressure on end strength goes down, we're—we all spend over 50 cents of our dollar on our people, the most important weapon system that we have. In the Marine Corps, it happens to be about 61 cents on the dollar. We have also stood up cyber mission teams and cyber support teams, both for the service and for some of the geographic combatant commanders—in our particular case, Special Operations Command. So, then you get into the tension about providing conventional force capability and providing cyber capability. It really shouldn't be a tension. You should provide both. But, when you're under an end-strength reduction and a fiscal reduction, that's hard to do.

General SPENCER. Yes, Senator, and we're similar. We've got 20 cyber teams, growing to 40, as General Allyn mentioned. Because of funding, we've had to stretch that out longer than we would—we're comfortable with.

You know, I was raised, you know, to keep my personal business to myself. You know, my daughter puts all of her business out on Facebook. I don't really get that.

[Laughter.]

General SPENCER. But, that's kind of the generation of folks that are coming in the military now, that everything they do and everywhere they go and everything they eat and everybody they talk to is on Facebook. You know, we're realizing now, that's a vulnerability. So, all of us have—you know, all of the names that were listed by ISIL on their list, we've contacted them all and talked to them specifically about these sort of social networks, if you will, that they put your—you know, your access out there. Unfortunately for us, I mean, you can Google any of us, and our whole life history is out there, whether we like it or not. But, for a lot of our troops that deploy, again, those, you know, Twitter or Facebook, all those—they're great social tools, but they also make us all vulnerable, and they expose our personal—some of our personal information.

Senator AYOTTE. Thank you, I think all three of us can relate to that, certainly.

I wanted to call on Senator Rounds for a brief follow-up question, and then I'm going to turn it over to Senator Shaheen.

Senator ROUNDS. Thank you, and I'll try to make this brief. It's just a followup to what the Chairman was asking about a little bit.

In terms of your overseas operation or your downrange operations, particularly with regard to ISR, have you seen any kind of a degradation with either regard to the cyber capabilities or your space capabilities? Anything, in terms of the items there that you would like to address or that you see as threats to our capabilities, that we should be aware of, in terms of things that impact your ability to deliver?

General ALLYN. Well, I think we have to be careful, in terms of, you know, just how much we can talk about, there is—

Senator ROUNDS. If a simple "yes" is there, then—

General ALLYN. There is risk out there in that domain.

Admiral HOWARD. Senator, I'm sure you're aware, for the Navy, we had, a year and a half ago, multiple simultaneous intrusions into our network. So, that really, I think, raised our awareness and our focus on defending our networks and making sure we mitigate risk in this domain.

Senator ROUNDS. Impacted you overseas.

Admiral HOWARD. It was simultaneous, and several different organizations.

Senator ROUNDS. Thank you.

General PAXTON. Yes, sir, there is risk. There has been intrusion and threat. We need both the policies and the monies to do the training to combat that, sir.

Senator ROUNDS. Thank you.

General SPENCER. Senator, I agree, and would offer that we could—any of us, certainly the Air Force, would like to come and brief you, sort of, one on one, if we could.

Senator ROUNDS. Thank you.

Senator AYOTTE. Senator Shaheen.

Senator SHAHEEN. Thank you, Madam Chair.

Thank you all very much for your service and for being here today.

I know this—I don't think the Chair has asked this question, though I know she's very interested in it, as well. One of the things that I have heard from folks at the Portsmouth Naval Shipyard, which, of course, is one of the shipyards that we're very interested in, is that if sequestration returns, the ability to attract the workers that we need for the shipyard is going to be compromised. Right now, they're in the process of hiring 700 people. We're seeing a whole generation of engineers, technicians, people who have real expertise at the shipyard who are retiring. If—can you just talk about what the potential challenges are, if sequestration returns in

2016, to being able to attract the workforce we need to fill our public shipyards?

Admiral HOWARD. Yes, ma'am. So, when I was down at fleet—this is anecdotal, but—as we sequestered and then we had a hiring freeze, and then we ended up furloughing different folks, we found, in some areas, that folks who had sufficient years decided to retire early, that the potential of not having a full year of employment, year to year, was enough for them to rethink.

So, for us, if that happens again and then we have to reduce maintenance contracts or make similar tough choices, in particular for our shipyards, we have that—a demographic, where we have an older cohort that's a substantial part of the workforce that might make that decision.

The next thing is, for the folks who stay, there becomes doubt as to—and a lack of trust as to whether they are going to have a full year's worth of employment. It's not just the pay. There is that component, because they have to support their families.

Senator SHAHEEN. Right.

Admiral HOWARD. But, it's also, they take a lot of pride in who they are and what they do as helping generate forces for our Navy or as public servants in other areas.

Senator SHAHEEN. Is this something that the rest of you are seeing in a different way as you're trying to recruit folks?

General ALLYN. Well, I think, ma'am, the impact of the furlough across our civilian workers was devastating. It gets at this issue of erosion of trust. We've got incredibly dedicated workforce, in uniform and in civilian workforce. But, there is a limit to, you know, how many times we can keep going back and asking them to hang in there with us. We have seen a similar case, where some of them that were retirement-eligible or could take an early retirement option decided, "You know, this has been a great run. I love serving in the Army, but I'm not sure the Army loves me as much as I love it." That's a terrible feeling for us, who take this on as a profession.

General PAXTON. Senator Shaheen, if I may, just as a overview of our civilian workforce, most of us are pretty lean in the civilian workforce. Between mil-to-civ conversions and then outsourcing and contractors, our civilian workforce has been getting smaller and smaller. The furlough and the BCA caps had a disproportionate effect on our civilian workforce. So, there is a sense of an erosion of trust and confidence, and they're really valuable members of the team. When the Commandant testified in front of the full committee several weeks ago, he said that, in the Marine Corps' case, only 1 in 10 in civilian workers, civilian in military is the workforce—over 90 percent of them work outside of the national capital region. So, there's this perception there that maybe the headquarters are bloated and there's a lot in Washington. Now, they're actually tooth and not tail, and they're actually out there doing important things for the service and for the Nation.

The anecdotal story that I bring up is, I went down our depot in Albany, Georgia, about a year ago, and this was in the aftermath of the furlough. We had worked very hard to keep folks there. Some of these folks are working in a very small county, a very rural county. The other two or three industries in the county, a rubber and tire plant and a golf plant, had left. So, the only viable workforce in—major in the area now, is—there's one health system and then there's the Marine Logistics Depot. When we started to furlough people, there was no other place for them to go. Many of them were working on equipment where they needed a security clearance. As they went from payday to payday without a security clearance, they were deathly worried that the creditors would come after them; and then, the minute the creditor came after them, even if it was a delayed payment in a home mortgage, that would affect their clearance, so that, even when the furlough was relieved, we couldn't hire them back because then they'd be flagged as a security risk. So, there's this horrible downward spiral when that happens.

Thank you.

Senator SHAHEEN. Thank you.

General SPENCER. Senator, we have a similar story. We also have 96 percent of our civilians that work outside of the national capital region, so at our training bases, for example, where we train pilots to fly, the entire flight-line maintenance operation are civilians, the whole unit. So, if you think about the Air Force—as an example, when we sequestered, last—or a year and a half or so ago, we stopped flying airplanes, we actually put airplanes down, which meant now pilots can't train, so they lose their certification over time, maintenance folks have nothing to work on, and airplanes— I happen to have a '72 Monte Carlo at home, and if you don't start that thing about once a week and drive it, it's not any good. Airplane—you have to fly airplanes to have them efficient.

So, we had airplanes sitting down. Now they're not going to the depot. Now you've got this stackup. You've got—don't have airplanes available. As you know, it's going to take X number of days to get an airplane through the depot. So, now they back up. So, it's not like if sequestration is suddenly lifted, you know, everything works well. No. You've got this backlog that you have to now push through a funnel.

The final thing I'll mentioned, that General Paxton touched on, is my son, who works for the government—he's a computer science guy—he—when we furloughed him, he—and this is similar to what I heard from a lot of other civilians—he was really frustrated, because—he said, "I can go work somewhere else and make more money. I want to be a part of the government." But, he said, "If they're going to—I've got a family. And I"—you know, two of my grandkids—"and if every time there's budget dispute, they lay me off," he said, "I don't know if I could do that for the long term." So, it had—it took a real toll.

Senator SHAHEEN. I very much appreciate what you all are saying. I think it's an important reminder for those who say, "Well, you know, we exempted uniformed personnel, and so it didn't have the kind of impact," that all of you are pointing out that it really did. Hopefully, we will act with more sanity in this budget cycle.

Thank you all very much.

Senator AYOTTE. I just have a couple of follow-ups, but, since I have my colleague, Senator Shaheen, here, I know she'd want me to follow this one up with General Spencer.

Just wanted to check in on the KC–46As delivery to Pease in 2018. I know there were a couple of testing delays, but are things looking pretty good, on track?

General SPENCER. Yes, Madam Chair. We're on track. As you know, we had a couple of concerns, but we are still on track. We had some slack built in. Some of—a lot of that slack's been taken up now. But, as we stand today, we're still on track. We still feel good about the schedule.

Senator AYOTTE. Excellent. Appreciate that. We appreciated General Welsh's recent visit to Pease, as well. That was terrific, and I know it meant a lot to those in our Guard and those that are part of the 157th Air Refueling Wing. So, please pass our gratitude on.

Senator SHAHEEN. Thank you, Madam Chair. We like to tag team on this issue whenever possible.

[Laughter.]

Senator AYOTTE. I just have a couple of follow-up questions.

One, General Spencer, I had a question about the joint terminal attack controller (JTAC) training, because recently it was brought to our attention, a memo that was dated February 25th, 2014, signed by the Commander of the 18th Air Support Operations Group, ASOG, Commander. The memo relates to JTAC training. The issue raised in the memo are problems with ground force commander coordination, airspace deconfliction, and nine line errors. The Commander also writes that an increasing lack of live-fly close air support (CAS) training opportunities and funds for temporary duties (TDYs) have eroded overall JTAC proficiency across the 18 ASOG. The Commander notes that continued decrease in the amount of live-fly CAS controls available to unit JTACs; and to the credit of the Commander, he intends to offset that decline with using simulators. So, can you give me a sense of what's happening with the JTAC training, and especially live-fly CAS training, and where we are with that, and just an update on how the JTAC training is going?

General SPENCER. Yeah. First, Madam Chair, I have to apologize. I haven't seen that letter, so I would like to go back and take a look at it and give you a more—give you a better response—

Senator AYOTTE. Sure.

General SPENCER.—so I can get the specifics. I'm actually going down to Pope Air Force Base on Monday to talk to some of our—

Senator AYOTTE. Okay. Well—

General SPENCER.—JTACs—

Senator AYOTTE.—we're happy to get it for you, and we'll be happy—

General SPENCER. Okay. So, if—

Senator AYOTTE.—if you want to take it for the record and get back—

General SPENCER. So, if I could, I would like to give you—

Senator AYOTTE. Absolutely.

General SPENCER.—make sure I give you a good response on that.

[The information referred to follows:]

JOINT TERMINAL ATTACK CONTROLLER (JTAC) TRAINING

Question. I just have a couple of follow-up questions. One, General Spencer, I had a question about JTAC training because recently, it was brought to our attention a memo that was dated February 25, 2014, signed by the commander of the 18th Air Support Operations Group, ASOG Commander, and the memo relates to JTAC training. The issues raised in the memo are problems with ground force commander coordination airspace deconfliction and nine line errors, and the commander also writes that an increasing lack of live fly CAS training opportunities and funds for T.D.Y. have eroded overall JTAC proficiency across the 18 ASOG. The commander notes that continued decrease in the amount of live fly CAS controls (available unit) JTAC, and to the credit of the commander, he intends to offset that decline with using simulators. So can you give me a sense of what's happening with the JTAC training especially live fly CAS training and where we are with that and just an update on how the JTAC training is going.

Answer. The 18th Air Support Operations Group (18 ASOG) is trained, combat mission ready and has certified personnel deployed down range. Regarding JTAC training, while we anticipate simulation to become a more significant element of our overall training program, we recognize that live-fly training will remain an essential tool for our overall combat readiness. By design, the actual amount of live-fly close air support controls for JTACs is planned to steadily decline over the years and transition to a more balanced combination of live-fly events and simulators. The Air Force is a contributing member of the Joint Staff J6 led Joint Fire Support Executive Steering Committee (JFS ESC). The JFS ESC produces an Action Plan which focuses analytical efforts and solution recommendations to assist Services and Combatant Commands in providing enhanced, jointly integrated, interoperable and cost efficient JFS capabilities to the warfighter. We collaborated with the JFS ESC to develop and field a Joint Terminal Control Training and Rehearsal System that provides a realistic, modular, upgradeable and scalable Joint Combat Air Support training / rehearsal simulation system. Simulation is already becoming a fundamental part of JTAC training. In fact, simulation is better than live-fly training in many areas. For example, simulation can permit more complex mission scenarios with more simulated aircraft involved resulting in a significant cost savings. The 18 ASOG is scheduled to receive a JTAC Dome simulator in the summer of 2015.

Senator AYOTTE. No problem. Appreciate that very much.

The other question that I had for you was, you know, about what's happening at Nellis. Can you confirm for me whether the Air Force has made a decision to close the A–10 Division at 422 Test and Evaluation Squadron at Nellis? If so—I mean, yes or no. I don't know if you're making that decision or where things are.

General SPENCER. Yeah, that—again, I'm a deer in the headlights on that one, as well. You—close the squadron?

Senator AYOTTE. Yes.

General SPENCER. No, I—again, I'll have to follow up with that, because I—

Senator AYOTTE. Then why don't I give you a follow-up question—

General SPENCER. Okay.

Senator AYOTTE.—on that one, too.

General SPENCER. Okay.

Senator AYOTTE. That's pretty specific.

[The information referred to follows:]

A-10 SQUADRON AT NELLIS AFB

Question. The other question that I had for you was you know about what's happening at Nellis, can you confirm for me whether the Air Force has made a decision to close the A–10 division at 422nd Tests and Evaluation Squadron at Nellis. If so, it would be yes or no, I don't know, if you're making that decision or where things are.

Answer. Yes. The FY16 PB divests the A–10 division at the 422nd Tests and Evaluation Squadron in fiscal year 2016. However, because of the prohibition on the divestiture of A–10s contained in the fiscal year 2015 NDAA, the Air Force will not be divesting A–10s at Nellis AFB at this time.

Senator AYOTTE. I wanted to thank you, Admiral Howard. You and I talked about this when we met in person, and that is on the maintenance projects at the Portsmouth Naval Shipyard. Frankly, you know, I want to commend the Navy for meeting and exceeding its capital investment requirements across all the shipyards. The thing that you and I talked about was the P–266 project at Portsmouth. I know I was very happy with your answer, and you're very focused on seeing that go forward. So, thank you for that.

Admiral HOWARD. Yes, ma'am. Thank you.

Senator AYOTTE. Terrific.

Not to keep you all too much longer, but there was one question that I just wanted to follow up since I had you all here, because I think it's important. You know, we spent a lot of last year talking about how are we going to address sexual assaults in the military. Having all of you here today, I think I'd be remiss if I didn't ask you how things were going, where is the status of—what's the status of the legislation that we passed, and how do you perceive the implementation of that legislation in your branches, and—give us an update on how things are going and where you see we can help some more.

General ALLYN. I'll start, Madam Chair.

First of all, we have made significant headway in eliminating the threat and the presence of sexual assault and sexual harassment in the military. Most promising is that reporting is up. Our soldiers are reporting over 90-percent confidence that, if they report an incident, that the chain of command is going to take the right actions, both to protect the person that is—has been assaulted, as well as to ensure accountability of those who perpetrate the alleged assault.

So, we are continuing a rising level of reporting. We are seeing a reduction in the incidences of assaults. Both promising. But, we still have work to do, particularly in eliminating the risk and the perception of retaliation by our soldiers inside our formations. So, our sergeant major of the Army has initiated an effort called ''Not in My Squad,'' because the confidence level that we see at the battalion level and above is very high, but the incidents are occurring at the company level and below. So, he is bringing forward a group of staff sergeants from across our total force to get their input on how do we improve both ownership of resolving this threat to our trust and our dignity and respect in our formation, and accountability to ensure that every soldier, every leader, is doing everything they can, not only to prevent these acts, but to prevent even the perception of any—retaliation of any type.

We talked a bit ago about social media and the impact that that has. What we're seeing is, the most significant level, and the hardest to defeat, is the retaliation—the social retaliation by peers and others that's occurring in social media. So, we are arming our leaders with the tools that they need and the training to understand how to attack this part of the spectrum that is somewhat new to most of us, but, unfortunately, not new to our soldiers.

Admiral HOWARD. Thank you, Senator.

I'd like to, if I may, refer some of this to the report, but some of it to the conversations I've had with our sailors as I've traveled as Vice Chief. So, when I do my all-hands calls, I talk about this issue, about the RAND survey, and then ask them for their thoughts. Then, in particular, in San Diego, I was able to sit down with a group of 40 women who represent all the different communities on our ships, from commanding officers to the medical officers to engineers.

The—from the RAND survey, we understand that prevalence has decreased for both men and women. But, you asked, more specifically, what changes have we made, some of it based on law, that really has made a difference. The feedback I'm getting, which seems to be buttressed by the results of the survey, is, first of all, having Naval Criminal Investigative Service (NCIS) be the first one on scene to investigate sexual assault seems to be bring an objectivity to the whole process. So, that is an important change that—you know, I think all of the services are committed to professional investigation when there's an incident.

The—in our case, bringing in victim legal counsel—this is the person who's the—who helps the victim through the process—that person is making a big difference for our sailors and their trust in the—

Senator AYOTTE. That's music to my ears, because that was my piece, and I'm glad to hear that.

Admiral HOWARD. I actually just sat down with one of our first Victim's Legal Counsels. She's in Rota, Spain. She talked a lot about both her and the Sexual Assault Response Coordinator (SARC) and what their presence meant to the Victims throughout the process.

The other is, for the—for us—for the training, the bystander intervention. I've heard from our sailors, both men and women, and then it bears out in the metrics, that this training that we put together, the scenario-based training, really felt—empowered them to be able to take care of their shipmates. Then, when you look at the results of the RAND survey, that when our sailors saw something, nine out of ten of them took action. The training works. They understand the importance of taking care of shipmates, whether, when you see something, you go to help your shipmate, you help your shipmate make a report through another process, or you report it yourself. When I've spoken, particularly to the women, they say the training is very effective, but that the results are even more impressive. So, thank you for all of that.

General PAXTON. Thank you, Madam Chair.

I would echo—and I think the Secretary of Defense was on record as saying—in the subject of Sexual Assault Prevention and Response (SAPR), we have had almost unprecedented focus and significant success and accomplishments. We're not, as General Allyn said, anywhere near where we want to be, need to be, should be, but we're going to continue the focus. In the case of the Marine Corps, we've had almost 1,000 fewer documented cases of unwanted sexual contact. That's about a 30-percent reduction, so pretty significant.

The two pieces to your specific question that I'd like to highlight, if I may, Senator—number one is, there's over 70 pieces of legislation that have either been enacted or proposed, and it's going to take us a while to work with them. I would echo what the VCNO said. We have several documented cases where the victim's legal counsel office—or officer was a big help, both in comfort to the potential victim and then in the adjudication and the defense. But, we have also had cases, too, where we have now introduced a fourth lawyer into what was a three-lawyer equation, where you had a prosecutor, a defender, and a judge. You know much better than I, ma'am. But, we're going to have to work through that, because some of these cases will be challenged, and you would hate for the one out or the one each to perturb the goodness of the whole system.

The last piece, if I may, Senator, is just to highlight the centrality and the criticality of the commander in all this. We're very appreciative of the work by the committee to keep the commander involved. Because whether it comes to bystander intervention, NCO leadership, legal accountability, you have to have the commander there.

So, thank you.

General SPENCER. Madam Chair, similarly, we—because we all work together on this problem to share lessons learned, and working together to try to solve this problem. It's similar, the Air Force. Our prevalence is down by 25 percent, our reporting is up by 61 percent. So, we think that's all in the right direction. We've done a lot of work, as you know, through special victim's counsel, things to make sure victims are taken care of, make sure that commanders have the tools they need to prosecute if someone is found guilty.

Our big push right now is on prevention, preventing this from happening in the first place. So, we've done several things. About a month ago, we had a Sexual Assault Prevention Summit. We brought in everyone from E1 all the way up to wing commanders. We brought in experts around the country, brought in the Center for Disease Control. We spent a whole week diving into this issue. The good news was, the answer was yes, you can prevent it, but it takes a lot of study, a lot of understanding the crime and to have things that specifically get at it.

Just two weeks ago, I was down in North Carolina, in the Research Triangle. I met with folks from University of North Carolina and from Duke who are also working on this crime in their colleges—local colleges—have a lot of great ideas. We're partnering with them. In fact, they're on their way now to Sheppard Air Force Base to work with some of our trainees there. So, we're—this is something—I can promise you, this is something I—we all work on. I know I work on it every day. We're not going to stop until this is fixed.

Senator AYOTTE. Thank you. We're not going to stop, either. So, you know, I think this is something we—we did tremendous pieces of legislation and worked on this collectively in a bipartisan fashion in the last Congress. Now you've got, as General Paxton really pointed out, a lot of implementation of—you know, to get this right. I really appreciate what I hear most from all four of you, which is understanding the importance of this and the commitment that we need, you know, every day to get this right, and to work together on it. So, I appreciate your giving me an update on that. I look forward to continuing to work with you, all of you, on this issue.

Thank you all for being here today and for what you do for the country.

[Questions for the record with answers supplied follow:]

QUESTIONS SUBMITTED BY SENATOR KELLY AYOTTE

HOLLOW ARMY

1. Senator AYOTTE. General Allyn, what does a hollow Army look like?

General ALLYN. A hollow Army is characterized by prolonged and disproportionate investments across manpower, operations and maintenance, modernization, and procurement without corresponding adjustments to strategy. If we have too little of anyone of these, the Army won't be ready when called upon.

Specifically, a hollow Army is one that appears capable on the surface, but is unable to adequately meet national objectives without assuming an extremely high amount of risk. We accept a greater likelihood of forfeiting the decisive edge we expect our Soldiers to retain when we face an adversary in combat ... we create an opportunity for adversaries to experience a ''fair fight,'' which we should never permit given our National capacity.

2. Senator AYOTTE. General Allyn, what warning signs should we look for when we are coming dangerously close to a hollow Army?

General ALLYN. A hollow Army is characterized by prolonged and disproportionate investments across manpower, operations and maintenance, modernization, and procurement without corresponding adjustments to strategy.

By this measure, the Army is not hollow. However, we are beginning to see the warning signs. The Army today is able to produce only enough readiness to meet requirements—and we can only achieve this because of the extra funding made available by the Bipartisan Budget Act (BBA). The result has been a steady erosion of readiness across the force. Underfunding readiness not only reduces training, but the maintenance of our equipment as well. This is evidenced by a gradual decrease in equipment readiness. Because we are underfunding modernization, we risk our qualitative edge. Our equipment has continued to age, becoming less reliable and less survivable as the technological sophistication of our adversaries is increased. Finally, the underfunding of our installations impacts Soldier and Family quality of life and ultimately, retention. We've consistently deferred critical sustainment, restoration, and modernization projects, creating substandard living conditions on many of our bases. If sequestration levels of funding continue, we will have a hard time maintaining the balance between manpower, readiness, and modernization. That is a template for a hollow force.

3. Senator AYOTTE. General Allyn, would a return of defense sequestration in fiscal year 2016 result in a hollow Army?

General ALLYN. Not immediately, but the necessary actions to meet sequestration level funding requirements would keep the Army out of balance in terms of manpower, operations and maintenance, modernization, and procurement for several years—until at least fiscal year 2023. Without a major change in national strategy to account for a smaller force with reduced capability, the Army will likely experience a period where it is indeed hollow.

MARINE CORPS READINESS

4. Senator AYOTTE. General Paxton, in your prepared statement, you writes that ''approximately half of the Marine Corps' home station units are at an unacceptable level of readiness in their ability to execute wartime missions, respond to unexpected crises, and surge for major contingencies.'' What are the primary reasons for this reduced readiness?

General PAXTON. Resource shortfalls in available personnel and needed equipment at the unit level remain the principal detractors to achieving the level of readiness home station units need to execute wartime missions, respond to unexpected crises, and surge for major contingencies. The Marine Corps' principal concern going forward is the recovery of full spectrum readiness of our home station units and the reconstitution of the whole-of-force after over a decade of unprecedented sustained conflict.

The Marine Corps excels at meeting current operational requirements in support of the geographic combatant commanders. To maintain the high readiness of our forward deployed and forward engaged units, we globally source personnel and equipment from our home station units—the ready force. Ultimately, readiness comes at a cost and the high readiness of our forward deployed and forward engaged forces comes at the expense of our home station units' readiness.

Further compounding the recovery of full spectrum readiness for home station units is the paucity of available amphibious shipping essential to unit level training. Although Service-level training is protected through the future years defense plan, home station training enablers (primarily simulation systems and ranges, and operationally available amphibious ships) will steadily degrade due to inadequate sustainment, recapitalization, and modernization. Without appropriate funding, lower equipment maintenance levels will begin to quickly degrade those essential equipment pools, leading to degradation in training and readiness. Any reduction in amphibious ship maintenance will directly limit operationally available amphibious warships and erode readiness. Eventually, the equipment needed at home station will wear out; when it does, our Marines will lose associated training and therefore the proficiency necessary to keep these units ready to respond. Budget Control Act funding levels may force the Marine Corps to choose between having its home station units being either well-equipped or well-trained. Training home station units to standard is necessary since these units constitute the ready force that would immediately respond to unforeseen crises or major contingencies.

5. Senator AYOTTE. General Paxton, which type of Marine units are having the most readiness challenges?

General PAXTON. Approximately half of Marine Corps' home station units are insufficiently resourced to achieve those readiness levels needed to execute wartime missions, respond to unexpected crises, and surge for major contingencies. Using Marine aviation as an example in this era of fiscal austerity, Marine Corps operational requirements have increased while the overall number of Marine aircraft for tasking and training has decreased. Approximately 80 percent of Marine aviation lack the minimum required Ready Basic Aircraft to train to the minimum readiness levels. Lack of procurement (future readiness) and aging legacy aircraft negatively impact aircraft availability for training and meeting operational demands. A significant training and warfighting requirement gap of RBA exists. Shallow procurement ramps (not buying aircraft fast enough) directly increase both the cost and complexity of maintaining legacy systems beyond their projected life. Marine aviation is 106 aircraft short of the training requirement or 158 aircraft (10-squadron equivalent) short of the wartime formations. Out of 52 fully operational capable squadrons, 13 are deployed and 8 are preparing to deploy. Of the remaining 31 squadrons, 22 are below the minimum training level required to go to combat in the event of a contingency. The majority of the aircraft deficit is caused by insufficient aviation depot repair capacity and throughput. Our aviation depots have not fully recovered from the turmoil caused by the last sequester. Marine aviation is not sufficiently ready now; another sequester would prevent any opportunity to recover readiness.

6. Senator AYOTTE. General Paxton, how can Congress best help with these readiness challenges?

General PAXTON. The Marine Corps' current resource level represents the bare minimum at which it can meet the current Defense Strategic Guidance. This budget allows the Marine Corps to protect near-term readiness, but does so at the expense of long-term modernization and infrastructure, threatening an imbalance across the five Pillars of Readiness—high quality people, unit readiness, capacity to meet commanders' requirements, infrastructure sustainment, and equipment modernization. An extended imbalance among the Pillars leads to conditions that could hollow the force and create unacceptable risk for our national defense.

Congress' continued support, and specifically support of the fiscal year 2016 President's Budget request, will be critical to ensuring our ability to fulfill our commitments as outlined in the Defense Strategic Guidance. Further, an end to both the threat of a sequester and to the caps imposed by the Budget Control Act would allow the Marine Corps to begin to address some of the readiness imbalances and would introduce much-needed budget stability to allow for effective long range planning.

OPTIMAL ARMY SIZE

7. Senator AYOTTE. General Allyn, setting aside the budget-driven Army endstrength reduction currently being implemented, based on combatant commander requirements, what size of an Army do we really need? Active Component? Guard? Reserve?

General ALLYN. Assuming our planning assumptions are correct, the minimum end strength the Army requires to fully execute the 2012 Defense Strategic Guidance (DSG), and answer the current demands of the Combatant Commanders is

980,000 Soldiers, including 450,000 in the Active Army, 335,000 in the Army National Guard, and 195,000 in the Army Reserve. At these levels, all three components will be smaller than the pre-2001 force.

However, much like the Chief of Staff and the Secretary, I am concerned that our 2012 DSG assumptions may prove to be incorrect. The 2012 DSG makes a number of optimistic assumptions regarding the number, duration, location, and size of future conflicts. Today, we see requirements and operational environments that were not forecasted in the 2012 DSG. These include Russian aggression in Europe, the rise of ISIL, and the rapidly changing security environment in Eastern Asia. All of these developments challenge our assumptions and elevate our strategic risk. It is my military judgment that, based on increasing world instability, we should reconsider currently programmed reductions in Army endstrength.

IMPACTS OF BUDGET CUTS

8. Senator AYOTTE. General Allyn, Admiral Howard, General Paxton, and General Spencer, please describe how defense sequestration, combined with continuing resolutions, have had a lasting and negative impact on your Service's readiness.

General ALLYN. The readiness of the Army today is insufficient to support the national security objectives outlined in the guiding strategic documents and specified within Combatant Commander operational plans. Reduced funding coupled with sustained demand for Army forces results in fewer Army units available for contingency response and at lower levels of readiness. The specific readiness levels of units and the ability of the Army to execute its Title 10 requirements are classified; however, the causes and implications of the Army's degraded readiness are clear—over a decade of focus on counterinsurgency operations jeopardizes the Army's assured dominance to conduct Decisive Action in support of Unified Land Operations (DA/ULO). This degraded ability to provide sufficient ready forces to achieve those objectives outlined by the President has resulted in increased risk for the Nation.

Army readiness is approaching a tipping point. The combined effects of the Budget Control Act of 2011 (BCA), fiscal and end-strength reductions, and over a decade of conflict have suppressed the Army's ability to build readiness across our formations. While the Bipartisan Budget Act of 2013 (BBA) provided additional readiness funding, continued improvement requires multi-year consistent and predictable funding designed to build Army readiness beyond counter-insurgency towards decisive action in support of unified land operations. Sequestration will not provide sufficient funding to man, equip, sustain, and train units to the appropriate readiness levels and places our Soldiers at risk when responding to unforecasted contingency operations. The use of continuing resolutions wreak havoc on Army readiness, modernization, and manpower. It makes long term planning difficult. As a result, we are forced to train sporadically, and the materiel and equipment we buy costs more and takes longer to acquire.

Admiral HOWARD. Sequestration, the Continuing Resolution in fiscal year 2013, and a decade of combat operations have created maintenance backlogs that have prevented us from getting ships back to the Fleet on time and aircraft back on the flight line. We continue our efforts to rebuild the workforce in our public depots—both at shipyards and aviation Fleet Readiness Centers—and reduce the number of lost operational days, but it will take years to fully recover our readiness.

General PAXTON. For the last few years the Department of Defense, along with all other federal departments and agencies, has had to operate in an uncertain fiscal environment shaped by sequestration threats, BCA caps, and the near certainty of starting every fiscal year under a continuing resolution. Against this chaotic background the Marine Corps has been forced to make extremely difficult fiscal decisions that directly impact day-to-day operations. The recent budget cuts and the looming threat of sequestration have been particularly difficult to absorb. Today, approximately half of the Marine Corps' home station units are at an unacceptable level of readiness. Investment in the future is less than what is required, and infrastructure sustainment is budgeted below the Department of Defense standard. The Marine Corps has significantly reduced many of the programs that have helped to maintain morale and family readiness through over a decade of war. Additionally, the deployment-to-dwell ratio is being maintained at a very challenging level. The operating forces are deploying for up to 7 months and returning home for 14 or less months before redeploying. These are some of the damages to date caused by sequestration and lower funding levels.

The fiscal year 2016 President's Budget is the bare bones budget for the Marine Corps that can meet the current Defense Strategic Guidance. The budget prioritizes near-term readiness at the expense of modernization and facilities. Another round of sequestration would force the Marine Corps to significantly degrade the readiness of our home station units, which is the Marine Corps' ready force to respond to crises or major combat operations. The fiscal challenges we face today will be further exacerbated by assuming even more risk in long-term modernization and infrastructure in order to maintain ready forces forward. This is not sustainable and degrades our capacity as the Nation's force-in-readiness.

Annual continuing resolutions, some lasting several months, will further complicate these concerns. The delay in receipt of funds, combined with the uncertainty over when and how much will finally be appropriated, can wreak havoc on contract award timelines and our participation in training exercises, and put us at risk of accruing additional costs in the long run. Furthermore, because CRs only fund agencies at prior year levels, critical programs may not be sustained.

General SPENCER. The Air Force has sought to protect readiness accounts under sequestration. Despite that, fiscal year 2013 sequestration has had a long-lasting negative impact on Air Force readiness. Prior to April of 2013, readiness levels were already low, predominantly due to constant global demand combined with a 20+ year steady decline in force structure. In 2013, as a result of sequestration, we were forced to ground 31 flying squadrons, cancel 8 exercises, and significantly curtail 8 more. Additionally, maintenance, repair, and upgrades to operational training ranges had to be deferred, degrading our ability to support high-end combat training. Individually, the training and professional development lost as a result of sequestration can never be recovered. Institutionally, it has taken 2 years to recover readiness to a point where still less than half of our fighter and bomber squadrons are full-spectrum ready. This is well short of Defense Strategic Guidance requirements. Restored funding will assist in re-building readiness, but the Air Force will also need relief from the current ops tempo and time to regain capabilities lost as a result of sequestration.

9. Senator AYOTTE. General Allyn, Admiral Howard, General Paxton, and General Spencer, if defense sequestration returns in fiscal year 2016, can we expect the negative readiness effects to last for many years?

General ALLYN. Yes. If sequestration levels of funding continue, the Army will be out of balance until at least fiscal year 2023 and will require at least 3 years thereafter to return to a state of full readiness, albeit with a much smaller Army.

Admiral HOWARD. Yes. Under sequestration there is no path to full readiness recovery to execute the required missions of the Defense Strategic Guidance (DSG). A return to sequestration in fiscal year 2016 would necessitate a revisit and revision of the defense strategy. The required cuts would force us to further delay critical warfighting capabilities, reduce readiness of forces needed for contingency responses, further downsize weapons capacity, and forego or stretch procurement of force structure as a last resort. While sequestration has caused significant near-term impacts, a return to sequestration in fiscal year 2016 would create further serious problems that would manifest across the years and be difficult from which to recover.

Assuming a stable budget and no major contingencies for the foreseeable future, I estimate that we will not recover from the maintenance backlogs until 2018 for Carrier Strike Groups and approximately 2020 for Amphibious Ready Groups. Sequestration would derail these readiness goals.

General PAXTON. Yes, the deleterious effects of another sequester would further compound the turmoil caused by the last sequester from which we still are trying to recover. We have yet to fully appreciate the cuts that have been made to date; however, sequestration has a chaotic effect on the force during a time of extraordinary challenges. Sequestration does not fund the optimally designed force of 186,800 active component required to meet the strategy. Sequestration prevents the Marine Corps from generating ready forces to meet operational requirements now and into the future. Sequestration equates to less force capacity; we would not have what is needed to fight in a major war. Essentially, all operational units would be committed for the war's duration with no relief and we would have very little left for crises that would occur in other parts of the world. Home station unit readiness and investments in infrastructure and modernization will continue to suffer as limited resources are prioritized to protect the near-term readiness of deployed units in harm's way. A return to sequestration-level funding with a force of 175,000 active component would equate to high risk. At this lower resource level, our units that deploy to combat would not be as well trained and would be slower arriving. This means that it will take longer to achieve our objectives and the human cost would be higher. This is what we mean when we say high risk.

General SPENCER. Yes. Individually, the training and professional development that would be lost as a result of sequestration can never be recovered. Readiness growth takes time and resources, readiness develops momentum slowly. Additionally, readiness in a small force can be lost very quickly when time and resources

are not available. Institutionally, under the Balanced Budget Act, it took 2 years
to recover readiness to a point somewhere near the pre-sequester level. Even so, still
less than half of our fighter and bomber squadrons are currently full-spectrum
ready. We can expect the same or worse for the foreseeable future if sequestration
returns.

10. Senator AYOTTE. General Allyn, Admiral Howard, General Paxton, and General Spencer, how long will it take to recover?

General ALLYN. Under sequestration, the Army will not be able to bring its manpower, operations and maintenance, modernization, and procurement expenditures into balance until at least fiscal year 2023 and will require at least an additional 3 years thereafter to return to full readiness. Meeting Combatant Commander requirements will force tough decisions about how much "surge capacity" we retain, and how little dwell time between deployments our units continue to absorb. Increased demands from Combatant Commanders will elevate stress on the force and the risk to meet contingency response requirements.

Admiral HOWARD. The fiscal year 2016 Navy budget submission is designed to continue our readiness recovery, reset the force and restore our required contingency operations capacity by 2020 while continuing to provide a sustainable forward presence. However, under a return to sequestration in fiscal year 2016 and beyond, there is no path to full readiness recovery to execute the required missions of the Defense Strategic Guidance (DSG). A revision of the defense strategy will be necessary.

General PAXTON. We have yet to fully appreciate the cuts that have been made to date by sequestration. A return to BCA-level spending would further delay readiness recovery. Another sequester would exacerbate the fiscal challenges we already face today and force significant challenges upon the Marine Corps. The months-long sequester of 2013 adversely impacted the aviation depots leading to the release of artisans whose skills have not been replicated, leading to maintenance backlogs and today's degraded operational readiness. The specter of another sequester, especially one that is more than just months-long, would only lead to compounding the deleterious effects brought about by the 2013 sequester. The time needed to recover readiness would exponentially exceed the duration of sequestration, for an experienced and proficient generation does not grow overnight. Today, approximately half of Marine Corps' home station units are insufficiently resourced to achieve those readiness levels needed to execute wartime missions, respond to unexpected crises, and surge for major contingencies. There is no recovery under sequestration. It would take many years to recover readiness once sequestration ends.

General SPENCER. The Air Force's current plan calls for a recovery to 80 percent readiness by the end of 2023. However, this plan was contingent on full Presidential Budget (PB) 2016 funding, Overseas Contingency Operations funding moved to baseline, and a reduction of operations tempo to allow for a 1:4 deployment-to-dwell level. Recovery is likely to be delayed at least 5 years if sequestration returns in fiscal year 2016.

UNFUNDED NEEDS

11. Senator AYOTTE. General Allyn, Admiral Howard, General Paxton, and General Spencer, what is the greatest need for your Services in respect to rebuilding readiness?

General ALLYN. The Army's greatest need is budget certainty. Building proficient and ready units requires a well-synchronized training plan supported by available manpower and ready equipment. Without certainty in funding, it is impossible to fully develop and source a training plan beyond the short term. Further, a lack of budget certainty prevents the Army from developing a modernization plan because we are uncertain how much or how long funding will continue to enable fielding of modernized capability.

Admiral HOWARD. Time and stable budgets are the most critical elements of Navy readiness recovery. A decade of combat operations and the resulting high operational tempo require a period of time for reset. With the additional impact of the Continuing Resolution and sequestration in fiscal year 2013, we have experienced significant delays. Further budget uncertainty will create additional setbacks to restoring our readiness.

The fiscal year 2016 Navy budget submission is balanced to continue on a path towards readiness recovery while sustaining the most critical procurement and modernization necessary to achieve a ready Navy in the future. The Navy unfunded priority list forwarded by the Secretary of Defense reflects the additional procurement and modernization funding that would improve future readiness with respect to Navy's ability to execute the Defense Strategic Guidance. However, none of those requirements are a higher priority than the balanced approach offered in our fiscal year 2016 budget submission.

General PAXTON. The Marine Corps views rebuilding readiness through the lens of institutional readiness. Institutional readiness consists of five pillars: (1) Capability and Capacity to Meet Combatant Commander Requirements, (2) Unit Readiness, (3) High Quality People, (4) Infrastructure Sustainment, and (5) Equipment Modernization. Currently, institutional readiness is out of balance. Achieving and sustaining balance across these pillars now and into the future is essential to rebuilding readiness. Balanced institutional readiness leads to the whole-of-force reconstitution after over a decade of unprecedented sustain conflict to meet current and future requirements. A budget that supports required end strength and equipment recapitalization and modernization is an essential component leading to balanced institutional readiness.

General SPENCER. The Air Force needs both time and resources to rebuild readiness. Currently, time is our greatest need to recover readiness. However, time available to train (generate readiness) is severely limited by ongoing rotational deployments. The next significant limitation to readiness growth is skilled manpower for maintenance and operations. In short, after years of force reductions, we have a supply-demand mismatch. Two possible solutions exist: reduce the number/length of deployments to sustainable levels or increase the Air Force capacity to meet rotational demand to permit readiness growth. On the resource side, any defense authorization below PB levels will prevent full recovery of readiness.

12. Senator AYOTTE. General Allyn, Admiral Howard, General Paxton, and General Spencer, what additional necessary capability are you lacking in the fiscal year 2016 budget?

General ALLYN. The Army's unfunded priorities list was provided directly to Congress by the Department of Defense on March 27, 2015.

Admiral HOWARD. PB–16 provides the minimum funding required to meet the missions articulated in the Defense Strategic Guidance and Quadrennial Defense Review. However, Navy had to accept risk in naval warfare systems' modernization, aircraft procurement, and air and missile defense capabilities to meet fiscal constraints. There are three warfare areas that could benefit from additional resources: 1) improve sensors and systems to defeat current and emerging air-to-air warfare and anti-ship cruise missile threats; 2) increase strike fighter, intelligence, surveillance and reconnaissance (ISR), and logistic aircraft capacity; and 3) improve undersea warfare sensors and fire control systems. A summary follows:

- Air-to-air Radio Frequency (RF) Kill Chain kits provide our aircraft the ability to counter sophisticated digital weapons and combat systems proliferated around the world today.
- Destroyer (DDG) combat system modernization will increase our capacity to meet Combatant Commander Ballistic Missile Defense (BMD) and Naval Integrated Fire Control-Counter Air (NIFC–CA) warfare needs (to defeat advanced missiles and strike/fighter aircraft).
- Surface Electronic Warfare Improvement Program (SEWIP Block II) will provide radar and communications signal intercept, and defeat anti-ship cruise missiles, enabling surface ships to operate in an anti-access environment.
- Submarine towed arrays are the most important sensors in our undersea warfare enterprise. Current inventory is inadequate to reliably meet global demand.
- Our legacy strike fighters (F/A–18A–D) are reaching end of life faster than planned due to use and wear. Improving the inventory of F/A–18F and F–35C aircraft will help reconcile a near term (2018–2020) strike fighter inventory capacity challenge, and longer term (2020–2035) strike fighter model balance within the carrier air wing.
- An additional MQ–4C (TRITON) would increase our capacity to respond to projected worldwide Combatant Commander ISR demand.
- C–40A aircraft fulfill a maritime logistics requirement, and provide short-notice high-priority cargo and passenger missions globally. Two additional aircraft will bring the fleet to the minimum wartime requirement of 17 aircraft to support execution of Combatant Commander operational plans.

General PAXTON. In addition to the fiscal year 2016 President's Budget request, the Department of Defense has submitted to Congress a consolidated list of the Services' unfunded priorities. The Marine Corps portion of this list totals $2.1 billion. Additional requirements include funding to enhance aviation readiness ($1.5 billion), funding for additional investments in critical training and weapon systems such as Networking on the Move, Javelin, and the Infantry Immersion Trainer ($412 million), and for high-priority construction projects ($167 million). These requirements do not supersede those laid out in the fiscal year 2016 President's Budget request.

General SPENCER. In the event congressional funding exceeds the level requested in the FY16 PB, the capabilities the Air Force would seek to acquire using the additional resources are identified in our fiscal year 2016 Unfunded Priorities List (UPL). Readiness is the highest priority on the UPL; this includes munitions, training, simulators, ranges, vehicle support, and equipment. The next priority is modifications for legacy fleets and programs supporting Combatant Commander requirements.

ARMY BRIGADE COMBAT TEAMS

13. Senator AYOTTE. General Allyn, if sequestration returns, what will specifically happen to the readiness of our Army Brigade Combat Teams?

General ALLYN. Sequestration will reduce the resources available for training and maintenance of units thereby reducing the readiness levels of our Brigade Combat Teams (BCTs). Under sequestration, the Army will struggle to maintain sufficient readiness to meet all of its current known requirements. The lack of funding and the need to dedicate resources to units filling current requirements will result in a degradation of readiness in every other unit, eliminating the Army's ability to rapidly respond to a contingency or other crisis. We will have fewer BCTs ready to respond to emerging crises and unforecasted demands.

14. Senator AYOTTE. General Allyn, General Odierno recently testified that "The unrelenting budget impasse has also compelled us to degrade readiness to historically low levels. Today, only 33 percent of our brigades are ready, when our sustained readiness rate should be closer to 70 percent." What is the primary reason for this degraded readiness: insufficient training, manning, or poorly maintained equipment?

General ALLYN. Generally, four factors drive unit readiness: availability of Soldiers, availability of equipment; equipment serviceability; and unit training. Currently, Soldier availability and training are the leading factors of degraded readiness. The combined effects of sustained demand for Army capabilities, fiscal reductions, and the friction associated with re-organizing of Brigade Combat Teams (BCT) and the associated downsizing of the force, impact Soldier availability and the training time needed to restore proficiency. Unpredictable funding creates an additional, preventable level of risk to deliver ready forces.

15. Senator AYOTTE. General Allyn, if sequestration continues, what percent of units would have degraded readiness?

General ALLYN. If sequestration continues, the Army will only be able to build sufficient readiness to meet current known requirements. All other units will experience varying levels of degradation in readiness, ranging from significant to severe.

COMBAT TRAINING CENTER ROTATIONS

16. Senator AYOTTE. General Allyn, can you elaborate on how many Combat Training Center (CTC) rotations would be cut if sequester were to occur in fiscal year 2016?

General ALLYN. The Combat Training Centers (CTCs) continue to be our Army's premier training venue. If sequester occurs in fiscal year 2016, the Army does not plan on cutting any of the scheduled rotations. The Army recognizes the value of a CTC rotation to a Brigade Combat Team not only in terms of maneuver training, but training in processes such as deployment, field maintenance, mission command, and leader development—training that cannot be accomplished at home station. As a result, the Army has elected to accept risk in home station training and readiness in order to preserve the ability to train these complex skills. However, the cuts imposed on home station training (HST) as a result of the sequester will result in many units arriving at the CTC in a degraded state of readiness—which means they will depart the CTC-experience less ready than a fully resourced HST model delivers.

PUBLIC SHIPYARD WORKERS

17. Senator AYOTTE. Admiral Howard, Admiral Greenert has testified that to address the workload to be completed in our public shipyards, the Navy will need to fund an additional workforce up to 33,500 Full Time Equivalent (FTEs) workers by fiscal year 2017. Secretary Sean Stackley stated that shipbuilding is critical to our security. If sequestration were to occur, how would that impact this Navy plan?

Admiral HOWARD. If sequestration returns in fiscal year 2016, it will force deep cuts to the Navy Operation and Maintenance account, impacting our ability to hire the public shipyard workforce needed to properly maintain and modernize our existing fleet of nuclear powered aircraft carriers and submarines. The resulting shortfall in shipyard capacity would drive delays in maintenance completion, negatively impacting the readiness of our forces, particularly those needed for contingency response, and diminish the ability to achieve platform expected service life. Ultimately, this puts our ability to provide the forces to support Combatant Commander requirements at risk.

It is also likely that continued sequestration would force us to forego or stretch procurement of ships and submarines. This would slow our progress toward achieving the 306-ship force required by the 2012 Force Structure Assessment and driven by the Defense Strategic Guidance. In addition, the resulting disruptions in the ship design and construction phases would have significant consequences for the health and sustainment of the shipbuilding industrial base, which relies on stability and predictability to cost effectively build the future fleet.

18. Senator AYOTTE. Admiral Howard, how crucial are these new hires to the Navy's readiness recovery?

Admiral HOWARD. Increasing the size of the workforce to meet the workload demand in the public shipyards is critical to ensure our ships and submarines receive required maintenance after many years of high operational tempo, achieve expected service life, and are modernized to keep pace with the evolving threat. Most of the work in the public shipyards involves nuclear-powered submarines and aircraft carriers, and there is very limited private sector capacity for this type of highly technical work. As a result, any shortfall in the public sector workforce capacity results in maintenance delays and deferrals, ultimately impacting Navy's ability to provide ready forces.

19. Senator AYOTTE. Admiral Howard, what is the work that will drive this demand?

Admiral HOWARD. The increasing workload in the public shipyards on our nuclear-powered ships is driven by a combination of midlife availabilities on our legacy ship classes and the first docking availabilities on our newer ship classes. Those include Engineered Overhauls on Los Angeles Class submarines, Engineering Refueling Overhauls on Ohio Class submarines, Extended Docking Selected Restricted Availabilities on Virginia Class submarines, and Planned Incremental Availabilities (PIA) and Docking PIAs on Nimitz Class aircraft carriers. The volume of this anticipated work is a function of these regularly scheduled yard periods and the growth work that has accumulated as a function of a decade of high tempo combat operations.

20. Senator AYOTTE. Admiral Howard, which shipyards will require this additional workforce?

Admiral HOWARD. All four public shipyards (Portsmouth, Norfolk, Puget Sound, and Pearl Harbor Naval Shipyards) require additional personnel to meet the projected workload in fiscal year 2016 and beyond

21. Senator AYOTTE. Admiral Howard, how will the increased need affect each of the four public shipyards?

Admiral HOWARD. Each public shipyard has unique requirements, based on their projected workload in fiscal year 2016 and beyond. The President's Budget for fiscal year 2016 supports these important increases, which began in fiscal year 2015. The total manpower levels by shipyard in fiscal years 2014–16, including both Direct and Reimbursable funded Full-Time Equivalents (FTEs), are as follows:

Shipyard	FY14 FTE Total	FY15 FTE Total	FY16 FTE Total	FY14 to FY16 FTE Difference
Norfolk	8,917	9,433	9,732	+815
Pearl Harbor	4,341	4,628	4,765	+424
Portsmouth	4,601	4,855	5,023	+422
Puget Sound	11,122	12,560	13,283	+2,161
TOTAL	28,981	31,476	32,803	+3,822

AMPHIBIOUS WARSHIPS SHORTFALL

22. Senator AYOTTE. Admiral Howard, of the current inventory of 31 amphibious warships, how many are prepared to embark marines and deploy right now?

Admiral HOWARD. We currently have two Amphibious Ready Groups deployed with assigned Marine Expeditionary Units. We maintain at least one additional Amphibious Ready Group for contingency response. Additional ships are capable of embarking Marines and/or their equipment and deploying as Amphibious Task Force (ATF) Lift. While specific numbers vary based on operational cycles, the total number of ships available for ATF Lift do not meet the full requirement of the Combatant Commanders.

23. Senator AYOTTE. General Paxton, what is the Marine Corps' requirement for amphibious warships?

General PAXTON. The Chief of Naval Operations and the Commandant of the Marine Corps have determined the force structure to support the deployment and employment of 2 MEBs simultaneously is 38 amphibious warfare ships. Understanding this requirement, in light of fiscal constraints faced by the nation, the Department of the Navy has agreed to sustain a minimum of 33 amphibious warfare ships. However, COCOM demand is more realistically defined at about 54.

It should be noted that, the 33 ship force accepts risk in the arrival of combat support and combat service support elements of the MEB, but has been determined to be adequate in meeting the needs of the naval force within today's fiscal limitations. This inventory level also provides the needed capacity for a forward presence and a MEB/Expeditionary Strike Group (ESG) to respond to a crisis or contingency within 25 days.

24. Senator AYOTTE. General Paxton, what is the impact of the shortfall?

General PAXTON. The Chief of Naval Operations and the Commandant of the Marine Corps have determined the force structure to support the deployment and employment of 2 MEBs simultaneously is 38 amphibious warfare ships. Understanding this requirement, in light of fiscal constraints faced by the nation, the Department of the Navy has agreed to sustain a minimum of 33 amphibious warfare ships. However, COCOM demands are more realistically defined at about 54.

Shortfalls in amphibious warship inventory have multiple negative effects. The 33 ship force accepts risk in the arrival of combat support and combat service support elements of the MEB, but has been determined to be adequate in meeting the needs of the naval force within today's fiscal limitations. This inventory level also provides the needed capacity for a forward presence and a MEB/Expeditionary Strike Group (ESG) to respond to a crisis or contingency within 25 days. Shortfalls also negatively affect our ability to train. Conducting amphibious operations with our joint services is not just a matter of putting Marines on Navy ships. Those units must have the opportunity to operate with each other during their workup to establish relationships, tactics, techniques, procedures, and build interoperability.

AIR FORCE MOBILIZATION AUTHORITY

25. Senator AYOTTE. General Spencer, Congress recently provided a new mobilization authority to give increased access to the Reserve components. To date, how many times has the Air Force made use of this new authority and what, if any, impact has this had on the readiness of Active component units?

General SPENCER. The Air Force has utilized 12304b to mobilize approximately 1350 airmen across a variety of mission sets in support of fiscal year 2015 Combatant Commander requirements. 12304b has primarily been used by the Air Force for pre-planned missions in support of a Combatant Commander when there is no other authorized mobilization authority (12302) available. The impact on the readiness of the Active Component is unknown at this time as the requirements filled by these mobilized reservists would have otherwise gone unfilled if the Reserve Component was not made available by mobilization. In other words, the Air Force did not have sufficient capacity in its Active Component force to fill all requirements levied upon it by the Combatant Commanders.

If the Air Force could change one aspect of the new authority it would be to relieve the Service of the requirement to provide prior notification of the use of 12304b in the "J-Books", and allow the service submission of the Program Objective Memorandum (POM) to OSD as sufficient notification. Due to the timing of the "supplemental" J-Book submission, the Air Force is not able to utilize the new authority for pre-planned Combatant Commander missions paid for out of the supplemental budget and still allow sufficient notification to the Reserve Component members to manage their employer and personal lives with enough time to deploy.

26. Senator AYOTTE. General Spencer, please provide deployment-to-dwell figures for Active and Reserve component units for each mission design series (MDS), i.e. type of aircraft, for 2012, 2013, and 2014.

General SPENCER. With a view towards regaining readiness by 2023, the Air Force manages our Combat Air Forces (CAF) fighter/bomber fleet at a 1:4 Deploy-to-Dwell (1:5 Mob-to-Dwell). All other MDS' are managed at 1:2 Deploy-to-Dwell (1:5 Mob-to-Dwell). Specific MDS' are listed below.

Combat Air Forces MDS	Component	FY12	FY13	FY14
B–1	Active	1:2.0	1:2.0	1:1.5
B–2	Active	N/A	N/A	N/A
B–52	Active	1:2.5	1:3.7	1:3.6
A–10C	Active	1:2.2	1:2.3	1:2.0
A–10C	ANG	1:20.0	N/A	N/A
A–10C	AFRC	1:30.0	N/A	1:7.5
F–15C	Active	1:17.6	1:7.3	1:4.4
F–15C	ANG	1:39.6	N/A	N/A
F–15E	Active	1:3.4	1:2.9	1:3.3
F–16C+/CM	Active	1:8.3	1:2.8	1:5.6
F–16C+/CM	ANG	1:14.6	1:22.7	1:21.5
F–16C+/CM	AFRC	N/A	N/A	1:8.6
F–16CJ	Active	1:4.2	1:2.9	1:2.8
F–16CJ	ANG	1:8.2	N/A	1:4.3
F–22	Active	1:6.4	1:7.0	1:1.6
HC–130	Active	1:1.1	1:2.8	1:2.0
HC–130	ANG	N/A	1:18.1	N/A
HC–130	AFRC	1:12.3	N/A	1:6.4
HH–60	Active	1:1.5	1:2.6	1:2.5
HH–60	ANG	1:7.9	1:10.3	N/A
HH–60	AFRC	1:7.1	N/A	1:7.0

CAF NOTES:
1. N/A means no contingency deployment for that MDS during that time frame.
2. CAF Deploy-to-Dwell ratio based on deployment of lead UTCs for each MDS.
3. Dwell is average for each CAF MDS deployment during specified fiscal year.
4. We do not track dwell for Low Supply/High Demand weapon systems such as E–3, E–8, EC–130H, RC–135, U–2, and SOF aircraft (includes Battlefield Airmen). Dwell is managed by individual crew position and can vary widely within a single unit.

Mobility Air Forces MDS	Component	CY12	CY13	CY14
C–17	Active	1:1.7	1:2.1	1:2.2
C–17	ANG	1:6.3	1:6.9	1:7.5
C–17	AFRC	1:7.5	1:10.3	1:11.4
C–5A/B/C	Active	1:2.3	1:4.7	1:5.3
C–5A/B/C	ANG	1:3.8	1:4.5	1:5.2
C–5A/B/C	AFRC	1:5.4	1:6.2	1:6.7
C–5M	Active	1:5.1	1:4.5	1:4.2
C–5M	AFRC	1:5.6	1:13.2	1:11.0
KC–135	Active	1:2.4	1:3.2	1:2.6
KC–135	ANG	1:5.7	1:6.0	1:6.5
KC–135	AFRC	1:5.2	1:5.3	1:6.8
KC–10	Active	1:2.2	1:2.6	1:2.3
KC–10	AFRC	1:5.9	1:10.0	1:13.1
C–130H	Active	1:3.3	1:2.7	1:3.3
C–130H	ANG	1:7.1	1:11.8	1:10.1
C–130H	AFRC	1:8.1	1:12.5	1:11.1
C–130J	Active	1:2.0	1:2.1	1:2.2
C–130J	ANG	1:57*	1:18.7	1:7.6
C–130J	AFRC	1:6.9	1:5.1	1:6.9

MAF NOTES:
1. * ANG units in transition from C–130H to C–130J.
2. MAF Deploy-to-Dwell: Ratio of time aircrews are on missions away from home supporting SECDEF-directed contingency taskings and TRANSCOM/HHQ-validated taskings vs. time at home station.
3. MAF Deploy-to-Dwell Calculation: Line qualified available aircrews divided by taskings minus one.

EQUIPMENT RESET

27. Senator AYOTTE. General Allyn, Admiral Howard, General Paxton, and General Spencer, what is the current status of our retrograde and reset efforts from Iraq and Afghanistan, and what equipment shortfalls would we face if we were forced to surge in the next 12 months?

General ALLYN.

Afghanistan Retrograde:

United States Forces-Afghanistan reported that as of 28 March 2015, there were ~6,900 pieces of Rolling Stock (RS) and ~10,000 Twenty-Foot Equivalent Units (TEU) of Non-Rolling Stock (NRS) in Afghanistan that includes both supply and ammunition stocks. Of this equipment, about 3,700 pieces of RS and roughly 1,250 TEUs of NRS belong to the Army. By the end of 2015, the current plan is to reduce these totals by approximately 25 percent from their current values through either retrograde, redeployment or divesture efforts. The vast majority of non-Army equipment is Contractor Managed, Government Owned (CMGO) equipment that will be divested of in Afghanistan. The Army currently plans to retrograde a total of about 2,900 pieces of RS and 1,000 TEUs of NRS and divest all remaining equipment.

Equipment shortfalls due to a surge would be contingent on the size and scope of the operation. The Army has Army Prepositioned Stocks (APS) and equipment strategically located in or near the theater of operation to support several contingency plans that may potentially mitigate equipment shortfalls and reduce strategic deployment of unit equipment.

Iraq Retrograde:

There are currently no major retrograde operations on going in Iraq. We are utilizing our Kuwait based APS equipment to support CENTCOM operations in Iraq.

Reset:

The Army programmed to reset ~41,000 major end items returning from Afghanistan in fiscal year 2015. However, ~4,600 of those items are still required to support the Resolute Support Mission (RSM) and will be reset once they are no longer required for operations.

Depending on the type of units and equipment required for a surge, the Army's programmed equipment Reset schedule may be delayed until the equipment is no longer required for operations and is again available for Reset.

Admiral HOWARD. Navy is resetting both ships and our ground Navy Expeditionary Combat Command (NECC) forces.

Reset of material readiness in carriers, surface combatants and amphibious ships, after over a decade of high tempo combat operations, requires $2.6B across the FYDP. The majority of the work should be completed by the end of fiscal year 2018. Some reset work will continue at lower levels through fiscal year 2020 because some of these platforms require the availability of a drydock to conduct lifecycle maintenance to achieve their expected service life (drydock maintenance is normally on an eight year cycle). The Navy OCO request for fiscal year 2016 includes $557M for this work.

Navy capacity to surge ships for contingency response remains constrained until this work is completed.

Retrograde for NECC equipment has been successfully executed with only a small percentage remaining (currently in transit). With OCO ($62M), Navy's fiscal year 2016 budget request supports reset requirements for all NECC Mine Resistant Ambush Protected (MRAP) and Medium Tactical Vehicle Replacement (MTVR) vehicles, including communications gear and improvised explosive device defeat system installations.

NECC forces could support a surge if required, but would be accepting risk related to the inventory of tactical vehicles until reset is completed in the beginning of fiscal year 2017. Upon completion of remaining equipment reset, NECC will be fully postured to support contingency response requirements when necessary.

General PAXTON. As a result of the continued support of Congress via OCO appropriations, the Marine Corps has been executing an aggressive ground equipment reset strategy to repair and return our OEF equipment to the Operating Forces as rapidly as possible. All Marine Corps equipment was withdrawn from Afghanistan in December 2014, and as of April 2015, all equipment has been returned to CONUS. To date, the Marine Corps is approximately 60 percent reset-complete and anticipates reset completion in fiscal year 2017.

Our reset effort is helping in two key ways; (1) Providing an opportunity to repair, replace or recapitalize war-torn equipment slated to remain in our inventory; and (2) producing positive readiness impacts for some of our key high-demand/low-density equipment items. For example, we expect to see measureable readiness increase in many of our radar, satellite communications and motor transport systems.

The Marine Corps is optimized and resourced for global crisis response, and we give priority to the equipping needs of deployed forces. To address equipping shortfalls in non-deployed units, the Marine Corps is undertaking a deliberate effort to right-size and balance our ground equipment inventory to support our future force structure and ensure equipment is optimally aligned to requirements. This "ground equipment optimization effort" will support reconstitution to properly scaled and balance force by fiscal year 2017.

General SPENCER. After years of effort, major Air Force retrograde actions are nearing completion. Still engaged in combat, the Air Force has leaned its footprint and is positioned to support its Afghanistan enduring commitment equipment levels. Regarding reset actions, we still face significant work ahead to realize a complete reset of equipment after years of sustained combat operations. Major Air Force weapon systems do not have typical one-time "reset" requirements. Our major aircraft and engines are sustained on an ongoing basis. Sustainment requirements are driven by various timing criteria including aircraft/engine cycles, life-limited parts, flying hours, etc. Such on-going sustainment activities underpin readiness. Our major reset areas such as aircraft procurement, ammunition and missile procurement, aerospace ground equipment, support equipment, basic expeditionary airfield resources, and vehicles continue to remain a high priority for the Air Force. However, depending on the nature of a surge, we would most likely exacerbate existing munitions shortfalls Air Force wide. Cross leveling between combatant commands would be required and could create risk to other operational plans. If the committee would like additional, more finite detail, we would be happy to provide a classified briefing upon your request.

NAVAL READINESS

28. Senator AYOTTE. Admiral Howard, in your written statement, you note that the Navy has only been able to keep one Carrier Strike Group and one Amphibious Readiness Group in the heightened readiness posture—just one third of the requirement. What have been the consequences of that shortfall?

Admiral HOWARD. CSGs and ARGs deliver a significant portion of our striking power, and we are committed to keeping, on average, three additional CSGs and three additional ARGs in a contingency response status, ready to deploy within 30 days to meet operation plans (OPLANs). However, if sequestered, we will prioritize the readiness of forces forward deployed at the expense of those in a contingency response status. We cannot do both. We will only be able to provide a response force of one CSG and one ARG. Our current OPLANs require a significantly more ready force than this reduced surge capacity can provide. Less contingency response capacity would mean higher casualties as wars are prolonged by the slow arrival of naval forces into a combat zone. Without the ability to respond rapidly enough, our forces possibly could arrive too late to affect the outcome of a fight.

29. Senator AYOTTE. Admiral Howard, is the Navy considering forward deploying any additional carriers to make up for the lost presence under the Optimized Fleet Response Plan?

Admiral HOWARD. The Navy continuously evaluates how best to position our naval forces overseas to meet evolving security environments, but we have no plans to forward deploy additional carriers at this time.

While carrier presence varies slightly from year to year, our overall carrier presence will increase from fiscal year 2015 to fiscal year 2016. Seven month deployments under OFRP are a sustainable goal that balances our requirement to generate ready forces, provides forward presence, gets us to stable maintenance cycles, and enables us to respond to contingencies.

30. Senator AYOTTE. Admiral Howard, how, if at all, is the Navy used to meet NATO missions?

Admiral HOWARD. The Navy provides support to a wide range of NATO missions. Specific rotational requirements are identified through the Global Force Management Allocation Plan (GFMAP). Additionally, other forces are offered in a "Notice to Move" (NTM) status. These forces are offered formally to NATO to be available within 30 days of an incident.

Specific examples of Navy support to NATO include:
- Surface combatants support to Operation Atlantic Sentry, which provides for the Ballistic Missile Defense (BMD) of Europe. This persistent presence is a gateway for future endeavors, including Aegis Ashore, and establishing an organic NATO BMD capability.

• We provide surface combatant and Maritime Patrol Aircraft support to Operation ACTIVE ENDEAVOR, the U.S.-NATO counter-terrorism operation.
• Surface combatants provide presence in the Black Sea under NATO auspices. For example, USS VICKSBURG is currently the command ship for Standing NATO Maritime Group 2 (SNMG–2) which provided presence in the Black Sea for nearly the whole month of March. SNMG–2 began operations in January, 2015, and will conclude this June.
• Commander, Naval Forces Europe is dual-hatted as a NATO Joint Force Command, Naples, coordinating NATO operations in Kosovo. Commander, SIXTH Fleet is also dual-hatted as Commander, Naval Striking and Support Forces NATO, in Lisbon, Portugal.
• We actively participate in NATO exercises: BALTOPS, TRIDENT JUNCTURE, MARINER, and MANTA. Additionally, we conduct bi-lateral exercises such as Joint Warrior, to strengthen our interoperability and tactics with our NATO partners.

Port visits and Distinguished Visitor embarks, such as USS THEODORE ROOSEVELT's recent visit to the United Kingdom and embarks of senior government officials from UK, Finland, Sweden, France, and Greece, also deepen ties with our NATO partners.

31. Senator AYOTTE. Admiral Howard, how does that affect the carrier presence that is required for combatant commander missions?

Admiral HOWARD. NATO has not requested carrier presence in fiscal year 2016, and Navy is not sourcing any NATO carrier presence in the SECDEF-approved fiscal year 2016 Global Force Management Allocation Plan.

TRAINING AND SIMULATION

32. Senator AYOTTE. General Allyn, Admiral Howard, General Paxton, and General Spencer, in 2013, training simulation accounts were severely cut due to sequestration, yet they can provide significant cost savings where trainees and long-term servicemembers can learn lessons that don't cost thousands of dollars each time a mistake is made. How do each of your Services plan to integrate simulators into your readiness and training agenda?

General ALLYN. Live, Virtual, Constructive, and Gaming capabilities are integral components of the Army Training Strategy. Use of simulations is integrated into Army training in two ways. First, simulations are specified in our Unit Training Models and units use virtual, gaming, or constructive simulations to execute building-block training events. Units move progressively from simulations based events to ''live'' events. Similarly, in Army schools, specific simulations are required in executing Programs of Instruction. Second, Commanders routinely use simulations to enhance their training. For example, units train Mission Command using simulations to reduce lower-echelon unit participation to save on operations and maintenance dollars. Further, aviation units use the Aviation Combined Arms Tactical Trainer (AVCATT) to practice aviation missions in a virtual environment prior to expending flying hours.

Admiral HOWARD. Navy has long recognized the criticality of integrating Modeling and Simulation (M&S) technology into Navy's training and readiness plans. M&S technology is a ''readiness enabler'', and supports Navy's mission to man, train and equip our forces.

As a result, Navy formally established the OPNAV Simulator Training Requirements Group (OSTRG), which reviews investment plans for simulator, Fleet Synthetic Training (FST) and Live, Virtual, and Constructive (LVC) Training, Joint National Training Capability (JNTC) programs, and assesses current capabilities and limitations. OSTRG leverages the Fleet Training Integration Panel (FTIP), and meets bi-annually to achieve cross-community, multi-mission synthetic training integration, and proposes live training events for simulator-based training. Individual platform and integrated simulator/training requirements are codified in Naval Training System Plans. Furthermore, Warfare Area Simulator Master Plans, updated during bi-annual FTIP symposiums, formulate capability-based requirements and acquisition strategies to expand simulator training. These plans consider legacy systems as candidates for modernization and reflect the development of a full range of simulators to support synthetic training. The OSTRG and its members focus on cost-effective solutions and leverage new technologies to meet readiness performance standards.

Since PB–14, OSTRG and FTIP members worked to develop the first OPNAV Simulator Master Plan (OSMP). The goal of the OSMP is to provide ready, responsive, and adaptive forces at tactical and operational levels, through a training continuum that balances simulated and live training events to improve warfighting readiness while reducing Total Ownership Cost. The OSMP translates validated and Fleet-approved integrated training requirements into integrated simulator training roadmaps; and prioritizes and recommends sourcing solutions for Navy's simulator, FST and LVC training requirements in support of both platform and warfare area readiness.

General PAXTON. There is no doubt that simulators provide a unique opportunity to provide realistic training opportunities that offset some of the costs associated with real-world training. These systems allow for varied training experiences, can minimize ammunition usage, and decrease logistical costs. In fact, the Commandant's Planning Guidance for 2015 specifically states that development and use of simulators remains a high priority for the service.

> "We will continue to support the fielding of systems that enhance our proficiency and safety in operating weapons and equipment. Our investment in training systems will reflect the priority we place on preparing for combat and be fully integrated with training and readiness standards. I expect all elements of the MAGTF to make extensive use of simulators where appropriate."

> -Gen. Joseph Dunford

However, as with other modernization efforts, we have had to defer some simulator development initiatives in order to prioritize near term readiness. We are currently funding simulator development and testing through individual system programs and supporting contracts. Due to the programming cycle, Fiscal Year 2018 will be the first opportunity to fund enduring integrated simulator capability.

Specifically, the Marine Corps Training and Education Command's (TECOM) Modeling and Simulation (M&S) Master Plan, Squad Immersive Training Environment (SITE), as well as the Live, Virtual, Constructive-Training Environment (LVC–TE) identify service requirements for simulators and simulations. These requirements are being addressed by TECOM. In conjunction with this we are continuing our efforts to integrate aviation systems with ground simulations to provide opportunities to conduct training that tests the full structure and capabilities of the Marine Air Ground Task Force (MAGTF).

General SPENCER. The Air Force uses aircrew simulators in most cases to augment or supplement live fly training as simulators cannot replace all live fly training. We focus most of our simulator effort on providing training in emergency procedures, contested and degraded ops, mission rehearsal and area denial, all items that are best suited for training in a controlled and secure virtual training environment. Simulators are an integral part of the Air Force readiness training objectives. Without high fidelity aircrew simulators readiness would quickly be reduced to unacceptable levels.

33. Senator AYOTTE. General Allyn, Admiral Howard, General Paxton, and General Spencer, what cost savings can the Services leverage from using simulation technology when preparing our Armed Forces?

General ALLYN. The Army maintains a large variety of training simulators allowing units to train at basic skills such as marksmanship, driving, tank gunnery, and aviation. Some are networked to several others allowing battalion task forces to simulate large scale maneuvers at reduced cost and equipment OPTEMPO.

These training simulators save the Army money when compared to live training as they require less operations and maintenance funds (e.g. tank track, ammunition, etc.). However, the cost of acquiring and then maintaining simulators offsets a considerable amount of these savings—these systems are costly. Simulators are used to provide baseline and some sustainment skills, and to rehearse complex actions in order to reduce risk to Soldiers. Ultimately, however, Soldiers must execute their training in a "real-world" environment—such as with live-fire exercises. While simulations are vital in building Soldier, Leader, and unit proficiency, they cannot replicate the complexity and critical human factors that arise in live, combined arms maneuver exercises against a thinking adversary.

Admiral HOWARD. The Navy continues to explore simulation technology opportunities to ultimately reduce operations and maintenance costs while sustaining, or improving, force readiness. Simulators are integrated into individual and team training, both as part of formal courses of instruction and crew preparation for at-sea operations. Simulator investments play a pivotal role in improving training proficiency and delivery. Life cycle costs of simulation are less than the overhaul, and preventive/corrective maintenance of the tactical equipment. Simulation can prevent personal injury as well as weapons damage, saving thousands of dollars as well as damage to personnel readiness.

Simulators normally operate at a fraction of the cost of operational equipment (e.g. operation of aviation simulators are normally 1/10 or less the cost of actual aircraft flying cost). In addition, simulators do not wear out or break high-valued equipment during routine training. This applies to all levels of training where simulators can be used. In some cases, lower fidelity devices can perform a large percentage of training tasks lowering total procurement cost of a training system.

General PAXTON. There is no doubt that simulators provide a unique opportunity to provide realistic training opportunities that offset some of the costs associated with real-world training. These systems allow for varied training experiences, can minimize ammunition usage, and decrease logistical costs. In fact, the Commandant's Planning Guidance for 2015 specifically states that development and use of simulators remains a high priority for the service.

> "We will continue to support the fielding of systems that enhance our proficiency and safety in operating weapons and equipment. Our investment in training systems will reflect the priority we place on preparing for combat and be fully integrated with training and readiness standards. I expect all elements of the MAGTF to make extensive use of simulators where appropriate."

> > -Gen. Joseph Dunford

However, as with other modernization efforts, we have had to defer some simulator development initiatives in order to prioritize near term readiness. We are currently funding simulator development and testing through individual system programs and supporting contracts. Due to the programming cycle, Fiscal Year 2018 will be the first opportunity to fund enduring integrated simulator capability.

Specifically, the Marine Corps Training and Education Command's (TECOM) Modeling and Simulation (M&S) Master Plan, Squad Immersive Training Environment (SITE), as well as the Live, Virtual, Constructive-Training Environment (LVC–TE) identify service requirements for simulators and simulations. These requirements are being addressed by TECOM. In conjunction with this we are continuing our efforts to integrate aviation systems with ground simulations to provide opportunities to conduct training that tests the full structure and capabilities of the Marine Air Ground Task Force (MAGTF).

General SPENCER. First and foremost, our number one priority is to sustain and enhance force readiness. We use simulation technology to maintain, sustain, enhance, supplement, and in some cases, replace training conducted in a live environment. The use of simulation technology may or may not result in direct cost savings, but should result in a more ready force. Therefore, we do not have an additional cost savings estimate beyond those that have already been programmed and budgeted.

Training is a key to force readiness and training for combat and other operational missions is an extremely complex endeavor. Sophisticated threat systems and advanced operational capabilities are driving an increased emphasis on the use of simulation technologies (Live, Virtual, and Constructive-Operational Training (LVC–OT) capabilities). As threat environments become more dense and more highly contested, our ability to simulate them in the live training environment is becoming increasingly difficult. Additionally, our fifth generation weapon systems are so advanced that challenging them in the live training environment while protecting their capabilities and tactics from exploitation is likewise becoming more and more problematic.

LVC–OT capabilities address these issues by providing solutions for increasing the value of live operational training, and simulating the live environment using concurrent, high-fidelity, networked training systems. Leveraging simulation technology significantly improves our readiness at a cost that would be otherwise unaffordable. We are working diligently to maximize the value of every training dollar by optimizing our LVC–OT capabilities.

34. Senator AYOTTE. General Allyn, Admiral Howard, General Paxton, and General Allyn, if sequestration does occur, will training simulators be cut similarly to the 2013 sequestration?

General ALLYN. The Army will seek to optimize its investments in training by balancing operational training investments, institutional investments, and simulations investments. All three areas will be impacted significantly by sequestration much as they were in 2013.

Admiral HOWARD. A return to sequestration in fiscal year 2016 would necessitate a revisit and revision of the Defense Strategic Guidance. Required cuts will force us to further delay critical warfighting capabilities, reduce readiness of forces needed for contingency response, further downsize weapons capacity, and forego or stretch procurement of ships and submarines as a last resort. We will be unable to mitigate the shortfalls like we did in fiscal year 2013 because we are still recovering from operating account shortfalls that were deferred to later years in the fiscal year

2013 FYDP. Our PB–16 budget represents the minimum funding necessary to execute the defense strategy. Sequestration impact to training simulators would come if we had to stretch or eliminate building new facilities or reduce training associated with generating ready forces in order to husband dollars.

General PAXTON. Despite the unique training opportunities afforded by simulation systems, such opportunities would, as with all training efforts across the Marine Corps, be affected by a sequester in fiscal year 2016. The fiscal year 2016 President's Budget request represents the bare minimum at which the Marine Corps can meet the current Defense Strategic Guidance. The Marine Corps would be forced to reduce or delay home station operations and maintenance activities in order to protect near-term readiness, forward deployed forces, and our capacity to meet COCOM demands under sequestration. Though no decisions have been made regarding specific reductions under an fiscal year 2016 sequester, advanced skills training and service level exercises would likely be scaled back accordingly, along with advanced training technologies, simulation systems training, and related activities. We would also assume additional risk in our modernization accounts, reducing the amount of investment funding available to develop and procure new systems.

General SPENCER. In 2013 due to sequestration, the Air Force was required to make several reductions in simulator operations and support. While we did not remove simulators or completely shut down simulator operations, the Air Force cancelled large virtual exercises, reduced travel funding for units not co-located with a simulator, and curtailed simulator sustainment funding. We don't yet know the specific training areas that will be impacted by any future sequestration actions. During any sequestration, the Air Force will balance training resources to meet fiscal constraints.

COMBATANT COMMANDER DEMAND

35. Senator AYOTTE. General Allyn, Admiral Howard, General Paxton, and General Spencer, what are the current mitigation plans and strategies to meet combatant commander demand until full readiness is recovered?

General ALLYN. The Army currently meets the majority of combatant commander requirements for forces. The Army has identified a ceiling to the Joint Staff that identifies an upper limit for overall demand that still permits Service readiness recovery. Above this ceiling, additional requirements would put service readiness recovery at risk. In the Global Force Management process, the Army identifies which additional requirements would be above the ceiling, the risks to sourcing those requirements, and risk mitigation plans. For planned requirements, these mitigation options include cancelling or delaying modernization programs and taking risk in services and infrastructure. For unplanned or contingency requirements, mitigation requires balancing between repurposing units from other missions, meeting deployment timelines, and the overall readiness of deploying units.

Admiral HOWARD. While we continue to source to capacity, the reality is we do not have sufficient force structure to meet all Combatant Commander (CCDR) demand. CCDRs must mitigate risk through judicious employment of allocated forces.

Risk is mitigated through the Global Force Management Allocation Plan (GFMAP), by allocating forces to the highest priority missions, and in coordination with the CCDRs, Joint Staff, and other Services, to ensure global mission requirements are executed at an acceptable level of risk.

General PAXTON.
- For the Marine Corps to create dwell time necessary to build the institutional readiness our nation requires from its 911 force both now and in the future, we will have to change how we provide forces to meet Geographic Combatant Commander (GCC) requirements.
- In the near term, your Marine Corps will be ready to respond to the nation's call; however, our capacity to respond may be severely diminished.
- By reducing the capacity, but not the capabilities of our forward deployed MAGTFs, we can create some trade space in personnel and resources necessary to improve institutional readiness.
- Reductions in unit capacity alone may be insufficient to improve D2D significantly and more importantly to optimize unit readiness. While requiring further study, anticipate each element of the MAGTF will require uniquely tailored solutions.
- By tailoring the MAGTF to the specific capabilities required by the Combatant Commanders, we can create the opportunity for the Marine Corps as a Service to regain readiness from over a decade of conflict. These readiness and recovery efforts will further allow the Marine Corps to provide a "ready force" to support the operations across ROMO.

General SPENCER. The Air Force is currently meeting combatant commander rotational demand with ready forces, and they are performing exceptionally well in Operations RESOLUTE SUPPORT and INHERENT RESOLVE. Unfortunately, this has come at the cost of likely sourcing the demands of the Defense Strategic Guidance with unready forces. We have successfully mitigated risk to rotational requirements at the expense of our broader National Military Strategy. We simply cannot mitigate all of the risk at our current capacity.

36. Senator AYOTTE. General Allyn, Admiral Howard, General Paxton, and General Spencer, have you established milestones or metrics to track the rebuilding of the readiness?

General ALLYN. Yes. The Army has developed a combination of metrics to evaluate our readiness recovery and force generation efforts. Those metrics consist of, but are not limited to, deploy-to-dwell ratios; aggregate demand for Army forces, including deploy-to-dwell, theater committed, or prepare to deploy units; combat training center unit preparedness results (or other major training event); and minimum floors of full spectrum readiness. By examining these and other variables, the Army accurately tracks readiness progress toward healthy, sustainable force generation levels.

Admiral HOWARD. Yes. Navy measures our current and projected operational output through the Fleet Response Plan Operational Availability (FRP Ao) metric. This measures "presence delivered" and "contingency response capacity" against a standard of sustainable levels of presence and the most demanding Combatant Commander Operational Plan for contingency response capacity. The CNO recently discussed the FRP metric of 2+3 Carrier Strike Groups (CSGs) as our goal which reflects a sustained global presence of 2 CSGs and 3 "ready to respond" within about 30 days. Across most of the Fleet, Navy will continue to be challenged through this year, particularly for contingency response capacity, and then slowly begin to recover FRP Ao levels through FY 2020 across the force.

Because our depot maintenance challenges are among the most critical aspects underpinning our readiness recovery, we are monitoring the hiring plans and output of both aviation depots and shipyards closely, adjusting as needed. We are investing not only in staffing, but also in workforce development, to achieve these goals.

General PAXTON. Yes. Service-level readiness systems and processes are informed by, and inform, the Chairman's Readiness System that codifies readiness reporting and assessment used to track the degree to which readiness is recovering or decaying.

Our metrics to monitor manning, equipment, and training levels, and assessment process provides near-term analysis of readiness of the Marine Corps' ability to execute operational plans and portend readiness to resourcing linkages.

The full weight of the Budget Control Act would preclude the Marine Corps from meeting its full statutory and regulatory obligations, and adequately prepare for the future. Under sustained sequestration for forces not deploying, the fuel, ammunition, and other support necessary for training would be reduced thus inhibiting our ability to provide fully-trained Marines and ready units to meet emerging crises or unexpected contingencies. We would see real impacts to all home station units, then our next-to-deploy and some deploy forces ... this constitutes the internal decay, the beginnings of the hollow force we have fought so hard to avoid.

Prior to the onset of sequestration and operational requirements supporting the New Normal, the Marine Corps was on a trajectory to reconstitute to a ready force by 2017. Regrettably, this is no longer the case. We have not fully recovered from the turmoil caused by the last sequester. Full recovery is frustrated by the specter of another. Another sequester would prevent any opportunity to further recover readiness.

General SPENCER. The Air Force has employed a readiness recovery model that assesses the five key "levers" of Air Force Readiness (deploy-to-dwell ratio, and four resource levers—flying hour program, critical skills availability, access to training resources, and weapons system sustainment). Additionally, the model provides an analytical assessment of 20 leading indicators of readiness to provide a detailed understanding of the range of possibilities for resourcing and ops tempo over the planning horizon. This methodology helps quantify two key readiness realities; the readiness generation process takes resources and time. While one lever cannot fix the problem independently, a shortfall in any single lever can create a severe readiness problem. Our readiness metrics are tracked through the Joint Service system called Defense Readiness Reporting System. This system communicates commanders' observations, concerns, metrics, and approaches to their combat readiness, from the field back to the headquarters staff. The aggregate findings from the field are shared with our legislators through the Quarterly Readiness Report to Congress. With that understanding, our requirements to achieve 80 percent readiness by the end of 2023 are PB-level funding of programs that support the four resource levers, in combination with improved deploy-to-dwell ratios for our force; through 2023.

37. Senator AYOTTE. General Allyn, Admiral Howard, General Paxton, and General Spencer, if sequester does happen, how many years would full readiness recovery be delayed, and how would you respond to the needs of combatant command?

General ALLYN. Under sequestration, the Army will not be able to bring its manpower, operations and maintenance, modernization, and procurement expenditures into balance until at least FY23 and will require at least an additional 3 years thereafter to return to full readiness. In short, the nation would be accepting considerable risk for no less than 7 years.

In order to meet the priority needs of combatant commands, the Army would focus resources on deploying units and decrement training resources for units not deploying. This will increase the risk for contingency operations and weaken overall leadership experience across the Army, but will ensure we can meet Combatant Commander near term requirements.

Admiral HOWARD. Under sequestration there is no path to full readiness recovery to execute the required missions of the Defense Strategic Guidance (DSG). Our PB16 budget submission represents the bare minimum necessary to execute the DSG in the world we face. A return to sequestration in fiscal year 2016 would necessitate a revisit and revision of the defense strategy.

In the short term, the required cuts would force us to further delay critical warfighting capabilities, reduce readiness of forces needed for contingency responses, further downsize weapons capacity, and forego or stretch procurement of force structure as a last resort. While sequestration causes significant near-term impacts, it would also create serious problems that would manifest themselves after 2020 and would be difficult to recover from. For example, even assuming a stable budget at PB–16 levels and no major contingencies for the foreseeable future, we estimate that Navy will not recover from the maintenance backlogs that have accumulated from the high operational tempo over the last decade of war and the additional effects of the fiscal year 2013 sequestration until approximately fiscal year 2018 for Carrier Strike Groups and approximately fiscal year 2020 for Amphibious Ready Groups, more than five years after sequestration in fiscal year 2013.

As we did in fiscal year 2013, if sequestered in 2016 and beyond, Navy will deliver ready forces forward to meet the highest priorities of the Combatant Commanders. Some lower priority deployments may have to be cancelled and contingency response capacity will continue at reduced levels.

General PAXTON. We are not able to fully assess the impact of a sequester or BCA funding levels. One of the greatest challenges with this current environment is the constant change and resultant uncertainty. We are providing our best estimates for all aspects of our Title X responsibilities, but we do know that we will have fewer units resulting in less capacity and high deployment to dwell ratios (Organize).

There will be reduced time to train, as well as reduced assets available for training (such as fuel, ammunition, and equipment readiness) (Train).

Reduced equipment availability and legacy equipment not on par with the modern battlefield (AAVs, 4th generation aircraft, outmoded radars and C4I) (Equip).

Over time, sequestered budgets will prevent the Marine Corps from meeting Combatant Commanders' requirements at an acceptable deployment to dwell ratio and prioritize training resources toward next to deploy units, leading to a less-ready force.

With respect to our response to a major contingency, all of the Marine Corps' operational units would be fully committed with no capacity for rotation of forces. Bottom line, those units directed to the operation would remain until the mission is complete regardless of the duration.

In the near term, your Marine Corps will be ready to respond to the nation's call; however, our capacity to respond will be severely diminished.

By tailoring the MAGTF to the specific capabilities required by the Combatant Commanders, we can create the opportunity for the Marine Corps as a Service to regain readiness from over a decade of conflict. This readiness and recovery model would allow the Marine Corps' home station units to be the ready force that would respond to unforeseen crises and major contingencies.

General SPENCER. The Air Force is committed to meeting Combatant Commander requirements for all aspects of Air Power projection. To that end we are performing exceptionally well in Operations RESOLUTE SUPPORT and INHERENT RESOLVE. If sequester were to return, we would likely continue to perform at high levels in support of these and similar operations, to the further detriment of overall full-spectrum readiness. Under sequester funding levels, our recovery rate to achieve 80 percent readiness by the end of 2023 would slow significantly; delaying this goal by at least 5 years. Finally, Combatant Commander requirements extend well beyond counterterrorism and counterinsurgency efforts and the Air Force is committed to supporting Combatant Commander needs were we to go to war with a near-peer adversary in a high-end fight. We would have insufficient ready forces to meet that demand and the requirements of the Defense Strategic Guidance.

SPECIAL PURPOSE MARINE AIR-GROUND TASK FORCE

38. Senator AYOTTE. General Paxton, in December 2014 testimony, General Dunford testified that approximately 50 percent of Marine Corps units at home station were in a degraded state of readiness due to personnel and equipment shortfalls. He further noted that this lack of readiness is due, in part, to the increased requirements from the unexpected Special Purpose Marine Air Ground Task Force (MAGTF) crisis response teams in U.S. Central Command (CENTCOM) and U.S. Africa Command (AFRICOM). Did the Force Structure Review Group consider the Special Purpose MAGTF crisis response team requirements when determining the optimal number of forces required? If not, how will this new—and potentially enduring—requirement affect the Marine Corps' ability to meet personnel tempo goals and readiness requirements as the size of the force continues to decline?

General PAXTON. No, the Force Structure Review Group did not consider the SPMAGTFs for CENTCOM or AFRICOM when it was originally convened. However, the 186,800 force was designed to optimally fulfill a crisis response capability which these units are performing. In a fiscally constrained environment below 186,800, since we are committed to maintaining near term readiness and crisis response, the enduring requirement for these units will negatively affect the readiness of home station units which are preparing for contingency response in support of Major Combat Operations (MCO). If we were fully funded at the optimal 186,800 personnel end strength we would be able to fulfill our crisis response capability and improve our preparedness for contingency response because the increased dwell time built into this end strength allows sufficient time to train, equip, and man home station units.

39. Senator AYOTTE. General Paxton, what is the Marine Corps doing to ensure we're not 'robbing Peter to pay Paul' when you remove capabilities and readiness from Marine Expeditionary Forces to stand up Special Purpose MAGTFs?

General PAXTON. The current construct of a three-ship Amphibious Ready Group (ARG) and a Marine Expeditionary Unit (MEU) remains America's preeminent crisis response force providing deterrence and decision space across the range of military operations. However, amphibious war ship inventory and operational tempo constrain the number of ARGs available to support Combatant Commanders. In a changing security environment, forward deployed and forward engaged Special Purpose MAGTFs are employed to provide crisis response, security, and theater cooperation capabilities as required by the Combatant Commanders. Special Purpose MAGTFs are intended to fill the crisis response gap when the paucity of operationally available amphibious warships precludes the allocation of ARG/MEUs to the Combatant Commanders.

The Marine Corps' top resourcing priority remains those forward deployed and forward engaged Marines and Marine units, especially those in harm's way. To protect the readiness of those forward deployed and forward engaged units—such as Special Purpose MAGTFs and Marine Expeditionary Units—personnel and equipment are resourced from home station units subordinate to the three Marine Expeditionary Forces. Home station units constitute the ready force that would surge to unforeseen crises and major contingencies. The Marine Corps is committed to generating ready forces to respond to all operational requirements, while working to ensure all Marine Expeditionary Forces are capable of executing missions. However, another sequester would prevent any opportunity to recover the readiness our Nation deserves and lead to creating a hollow force we have fought so hard to avoid. In a major conflict, resource shortfalls resulting from sequester-level funding would increase the timelines needed to achieve our objectives thus elevating the likelihood of mission failure and greater loss of life.

40. Senator AYOTTE. General Paxton, with approximately 50 percent of home station units, which are needed to respond to major crises, being declared "not ready", what is the Marine Corps' plan to restore these units to readiness?

General PAXTON. Home station units constitute the ready force that would respond to unforeseen crises and contingencies. As the Nation's ready force, the Marine Corps will continue to generate ready forces to meet current operational requirements, work to recover full spectrum readiness for home station units, and protect those aspects of institutional readiness that allow for the reconstitution of the whole-of-force after over a decade of unprecedented sustained conflict. Personnel shortfalls at the unit level are a principal detractor to recovering readiness. Actions taken to help restore home station unit readiness include manning assignment policies that improve (1) leader-to-led ratios, especially among the Noncommissioned Officer and Staff Noncommissioned Office grades; (2) required unit personnel fill levels essential for combat effectiveness, (3) seek to employ the force at a 1:3 deployment to dwell ratio (optimum) in the future, and(4) optimized readiness across the entire unit life cycle versus only the pre-deployment training period. The Marine Corps regularly examines balancing the requirements to meet current operational requirements against operational tempo that promotes readiness restoration of home station units.

41. Senator AYOTTE. General Paxton, what specific risks are the Marine Corps taking by having a total force less than the optimal force of 186,000?

General PAXTON. A discussion of required force structure to meet U.S. national security requirements must be viewed from the lens of the five pillars of readiness. At PB16 funding levels, the Marine Corps meets current crisis and contingency response force levels, but with some risk. We will meet the nation's requirements, the question is, how well can we prepare those troops for deployment? In order to make continuous and long term readiness a reality, we have to be able to train personnel and perform maintenance on equipment. Right now, we have about a 1:2 deployment to dwell ratio. That is, Marines are deployed for 7 months and home for 14. This allows a proper unit rotation to ensure that each time a unit deploys they are fully ready. If we are forced to take further cuts, that level will decrease closer to 1:1.5 or 1:1. What this means is that units have less time between deployments to conduct the required training prior to their next deployment.

JOINT LIGHT TACTICAL VEHICLE

42. Senator AYOTTE. General Allyn and General Paxton, how important is the Joint Light Tactical Vehicle (JLTV) program to the readiness of each of your Services?

General ALLYN. Joint Light Tactical Vehicle (JLTV) fielding will substantially improve Army readiness by closing capability gaps in the Army's light tactical vehicle fleet. Tactical mobility is a vital ground combat force enabler and enhances the effectiveness of combat and sustainment forces. The current High Mobility Multi-purpose Wheeled Vehicle (HMMWV) is not suitable in the current environment as armoring initiatives have overweighed the chassis, limiting its mobility. Additionally, the HMMWV lacks the requisite on-board power to support the current mission command systems. Current trends in military operations require forces to continue to develop expeditionary capabilities across the range of military operations. The JLTV provides the mobility Soldiers need, with the protection and on-board power needed in the future operating environment. The Mine-Resistant Ambush Protected (MRAP) vehicles used in Iraq and Afghanistan lacked the cross-country mobility JLTV will provide. MRAP's size and weight limited Army operations to road networks making our Soldiers' movements predictable and easier to target. JLTV will allow our Soldiers more flexibility for off-road operations, reducing their exposure to Improvised Explosive Devices and ambushes. This added mobility coupled with the increased protection integrated into the JLTV design reduces our Soldiers' risk. Finally, JLTV is designed to enable the integration of our current and future mission command. This will enable commanders to see the battlefield and synchronize combat power to enable mission success. The Army plans to prioritize early fielding to Infantry Brigades and Special Operations Forces.

General PAXTON. The JLTV is a central pillar of our ground combat and tactical vehicle modernization plan and critical to readiness of Marine Corps forces to deploy and to be employed in any clime and place. The JLTV program, and the capability it will provide, is second only in importance to our amphibious mobility modernization within our vehicle portfolio. JLTVs will replace the portion of HMMWVs that are most at risk; those that perform a combat function and are most likely to be exposed to enemy fires. Those vehicles are assigned predominately to Ground Combat Element and Direct Support Logistics units, and perform mission roles as Heavy Weapons (Machine Guns) and Anti-Armor (TOW and Javelin) Weapons carriers and critical command and control and tactical logistics functions.

Initially, we will procure and field 5,500 JLTVs between fiscal years 2017 and 2022, to replace the highest risk portion of our 18,000 vehicle HMMWV fleet. In addition to providing protection equivalent to the base MRAP All-Terrain Vehicle (M–ATV), the JLTV will restore off-road performance and payload to the light vehicle fleet that was lost when 'frag kit' armor was installed on HMMWVs during Operation Iraqi Freedom. Frag kit armor does not protect against the underbody IED threat, a major vulnerability of the HMMWV, and the reason why it could not be used in recent combat operations. The JLTV will support the most demanding missions, including Joint Forcible Entry and crisis response operations from the sea. The JLTV will be transportable externally by CH–53 helicopter and will be capable of being stored and transported in the spaces formerly occupied by HMMWVs aboard amphibious and maritime prepositioning ships and surface connectors, such as the LCAC. JLTV competitive prototypes have also demonstrated fuel efficiency equal to a similarly equipped HMMWV, while moving, and a 20 percent less fuel use when at idle.

We are pleased with the performance of the JLTV program and the three highly competitive vendors, AM General, Lockheed Martin, and Oshkosh Defense, working with us during the program's Engineering, and Manufacturing Development (EMD) phase. We look forward to working with our U. S. Army partners later this summer as the JLTV program prepares for its Milestone C decision and the selection of one of the EMD vendors to produce JLTV, beginning in fiscal year 2016.

43. Senator AYOTTE. General Allyn and General Paxton, as the JLTV program ramps up, how will existing HMMWV (Humvee) vehicles be reallocated?

General ALLYN. As the four JLTV variants (Heavy Gun Carrier, Close Combat Weapons Carrier, General Purpose, Utility/Shelter Carrier) are fielded to units, the Army will reallocate the most modern HMMWVs across all Army Components to replace older model HMMWVs. The Army will then divest those older model HMMWVs.

General PAXTON. Our intent is to replace the entire HMMWV fleet. Between 2017 and 2022 we will procure the first of the 5,500 JLTV's to replace the aging and over-burdened HMMWV fleet. These 5,500 will fulfill a portion of the overall requirement we have for roughly ~18,000 vehicles. JLTVs will replace the portion of HMMWVs that are most at risk; those that perform a combat function and are most likely to be exposed to enemy fires. Those vehicles are assigned predominately to Ground Combat Element and Direct Support Logistics units, and perform mission roles as Heavy Weapons (Machine Guns) and Anti-Armor (TOW and Javelin) Weapons carriers and critical command and control and tactical logistics functions.

The current Ground Combat Vehicle Strategy (GCTVS) outlines our plan to replace the remaining HMMWV fleet with JLTV, however we will need to make investments in the ACV during the 2020's to ensure that this platform remains prepared to carry us into the future. By sequencing our JLTV buy around the peak years of the ACV program, and modernizing a portion of our AAV fleet we will be able to achieve our long range goals within the projected limits of future budget restrictions. However, if the budget is fully sequestered in fiscal year 2016 or beyond, it will jeopardize both the timing and resources required to undertake this strategy and greatly affect our ability to achieve our requirements in both vehicle fleets.

44. Senator AYOTTE. General Allyn and General Paxton, after JLTV is fully implemented, how many HMMWV's will remain in each Service's inventory?

General ALLYN. The JLTV begins fielding in fiscal year 2018. Based on Force Structure projections for that year, fielding 49,099 JLTVs will leave 67,301 HMMWVs distributed across the Total Army.

General PAXTON. Our intent is to replace the entire HMMWV fleet. Between 2017 and 2022 we will procure the first of the 5,500 JLTV's to replace the aging and over-burdened HMMWV fleet. These 5,500 will fulfill a portion of the overall requirement we have for roughly ~18,000 vehicles. JLTVs will replace the portion of HMMWVs that are most at risk; those that perform a combat function and are most likely to be exposed to enemy fires. Those vehicles are assigned predominately to Ground Combat Element and Direct Support Logistics units, and perform mission roles as Heavy Weapons (Machine Guns) and Anti-Armor (TOW and Javelin) Weapons carriers and critical command and control and tactical logistics functions.

The current Ground Combat Vehicle Strategy (GCTVS) outlines our plan to replace the remaining HMMWV fleet with JLTV, however we will need to make investments in the ACV during the 2020's to ensure that this platform remains prepared to carry us into the future. By sequencing our JLTV buy around the peak years of the ACV program, and modernizing a portion of our AAV fleet we will be able to achieve our long range goals within the projected limits of future budget restrictions. However, if the budget is fully sequestered in fiscal year 2016 or beyond, it will jeopardize both the timing and resources required to undertake this strategy and greatly affect our ability to achieve our requirements in both vehicle fleets.

QUESTIONS SUBMITTED BY SENATOR TIM KAINE

SEQUESTRATION—SECOND AND THIRD ORDER EFFECTS

45. Senator KAINE. General Allyn, Admiral Howard, General Paxton, and General Spencer, in multiple hearings we have heard testimony from the Service Chiefs on

some of the negative effects of sequestration-level budget caps. In fiscal year 2013, the Services took varied approaches to implement sequestration cuts. The Army cancelled major training exercises, the Air Force grounded aircraft, and the Navy deferred maintenance. Deferring costs into future years can create second and third order negative such as creating training and readiness deficits and the loss of capabilities. We have not heard many details about these second and third order effects. Additionally, because of the focus on counterinsurgency (COIN) training to prepare for deployments to Iraq and Afghanistan, our military now has an entire generation of officer and enlisted personnel who have never conducted full-spectrum training. If sequestration remains in fiscal year 2016 and the Services again halts training for pilots, while they will continue to be paid, if they cannot fly—not only will they lose proficiency—but their morale suffers and can either lead them to leave the military or lead to behavior and family problems. Can each of you provide examples of the inefficient use of resources, such as time lost, increased long-term costs, and the second and third order problems those conditions create for training and readiness deficits?

General ALLYN. If we return to sequestration in fiscal year 2016, the Army will experience increased risk through degraded readiness to both our organizations and our installations.

Reductions to individual training and education will create a backlog that will take years to correct and create gaps at critical points in leader development—especially mid-career officers and NCOs. Unit training for approximately 80 percent of the Force will be curtailed, impacting basic warfighting skills and readiness posture, and inducing shortfalls across critical specialties such as aviation and intelligence. The Army will generate fewer Brigade Combat Teams (BCTs) to the readiness levels required to support rapid combat deployment as we balance the readiness levels of BCTs with other critical enablers such as Combat Aviation Brigades and Combat Sustainment Brigades. The remaining BCTs will be resourced only to minimum Individual/Crew/Squad levels. This will stretch the time required to flow forces into a war-fighting theater, allowing our adversary more time to prepare and inevitably leading to greater U.S. casualties.

From an installation perspective, our Army is still feeling the effects of sequestration in fiscal year 2013 when over 3.2 billion dollars of requirements were deferred to fiscal year 2014, to include significant Military Construction (MILCON) and Sustainment, Restoration and Modernization (SRM) projects. As you know, sustaining facilities is more cost effective than restoring them and our data shows that for every 1 dollar we purportedly 'save' on sustainment we incur 1.33 dollars of costs in restoration. By 2013, the Army already had a total restoration backlog of over 15 billion dollars. At current levels of funding, it will take approximately twenty-six years (2039) to return all of our installations to standard. A return to sequestration will only exacerbate this delay in providing our Soldiers and their Families with the mission essential facilities their selfless service warrants.

Likewise, a return to sequestration will compel the Army to defer vehicle maintenance. Under sequestration in fiscal year 2013, commands reduced OPTEMPO to make additional resources available to address the deferred maintenance workload. Additionally, the Army reduced the maintenance requirements from ''10/20 standards'' (all routine maintenance is executed and all deficiencies are repaired) to a Fully Mission Capable (FMC) plus safety standard, decreasing the quantity of reliable and deployable equipment.

Admiral HOWARD. Ship and air depot maintenance backlogs are good examples of the second and third order effects of sequestration. The impacts of the growing ship depot maintenance backlogs may not be immediately apparent, but will result in greater funding needs in the future to make up for the shortfalls each year and potentially more material casualty reports, impacting operations. For aviation depot maintenance, the growing backlog will result in more aircraft awaiting maintenance and fewer operational aircraft on the flight line for squadrons training for deployment. This will lead to less proficient aircrews, decreased combat effectiveness of naval air forces, and increased potential for flight and ground mishaps.

In addition, sequestration in fiscal year 2013 led to decreases in the workforce and overall productivity in the depots/shipyards due to hiring freezes at a time when the Navy should have been increasing the workforce to meet a growing workload and replace normal attrition. These outcomes were further exacerbated by workforce overtime restrictions which prevented recovery of production schedules. A third order effect was an increase in workforce attrition from accelerated retirements or pursuit of other employment. While difficult to measure motivation, the anecdotal evidence suggests that furloughs, lack of overtime and an uncertain future were key contributors to an increased loss of experienced workers. The end results were delayed and more costly shipyard maintenance availabilities, and aviation depots were unable to execute the necessary workload to keep the required numbers of aircraft on the flight line.

General PAXTON. A return to sequestration—or to BCA caps—would exacerbate current fiscal challenges and force us to assume greater risk in our capacity to meet long-term operational requirements. The Marine Corps' current resource level represents the bare minimum at which it can meet the current Defense Strategic Guidance. Though we are committed to generating ready, forward deployed forces, at BCA levels we will accept significantly greater risk in the next major theater war. This is a "one major combat operation," reduced-capacity force; essentially, we would be all in with no rotations, no surge capacity, and significantly reduced pre-deployment training. There would also be significant reductions in aviation and ground combat units, further reducing our available infantry battalions. Coupled with recent reductions in critical combat support capabilities such as artillery, tanks, and amphibious assault vehicles, such reductions would result in wars that last longer and extract a higher human cost.

At BCA levels we would be unable to meet our ongoing operational commitments and would forgo participation in many of our planned security cooperation exercises. Though we intend to preserve the Guam/DPRI effort as much as possible, a sequester would lengthen the timeline for completion.

In terms of lasting implications, sequestration caps would also require us to adopt massively inefficient business and operational practices that end up costing much more over the long term. For instance, delaying modernization in order to protect near-term readiness greatly risks driving up acquisition costs. Any interruptions during program acquisitions—schedule slips, loss of efficiencies, and potential Nunn-McCurdy breaches—would ultimately increase total program costs. Deferred modernization would have implications for our equipment maintenance programs as well. We would be forced to sustain legacy systems longer than planned, and to shift focus away from cheaper, more efficient green technologies, toward older, more inefficient and expensive technologies. We would also reduce regular, scheduled maintenance on ground equipment (such as depot-level vehicle overhauls) as a further near-term cost saving measure. However, the net result of this combination of obsolete technology and reduced maintenance will drive up operations and support costs over the long term.

We would see similar effects to our facilities. Long-terms infrastructure standards would be reduced, resulting in a score of Q3 or "Poor" on the Facility Conditions Index. Base operating functions such as utilities and services would be depressed to minimum levels, and energy efficiency projects would be eliminated. Over time the cumulative effects of deferred or canceled maintenance will accelerate the deterioration of buildings and drive up long term costs.

Finally, the return of sequestration would have costly implications for our workforce, particularly personnel at our maintenance centers. Because our depots are required to plan around the Services' maintenance funding levels, cuts to their maintenance budgets require corresponding reductions in staffing levels at the depots. This risks the accumulation of a maintenance backlog that must be worked down with (more costly) overtime. It also jeopardizes the retention of depot skilled artisans, thus permanently reducing our throughput/surge capacity. Our aviation units are experiencing these effects firsthand. The fiscal year 2013 sequester forced mass layoffs at aviation depots, which are now struggling to meet maintenance demands for our aircraft. The number of aviation assets available for training and missions has thus been reduced, and the readiness of our aviation units has dropped accordingly.

General SPENCER. Meeting the current and expanding demand for forces against a shrinking capacity has required the Air Force to make extraordinary choices in order to continue to supply air power. Examples of this problem manifest themselves in areas like remotely piloted aircraft (RPA) manning, fighter pilot manning, and maintenance support to flight operations. RPA pilot numbers are decreasing and RPA pilot training has been significantly constrained since 2007 due to the requirement to utilize RPA instructors for surge combat operations and not to conduct student training. The reduction of Air Force fighter cockpits limits the capacity to season junior fighter pilots, delays matriculation, and limits the experience level of our future fighter pilot leaders. Finally, reductions and limits to total Air Force manning have resulted in a lack of experienced aircraft maintenance expertise needed to keep aging legacy aircraft flying and to bring new weapons systems to active duty. Second and third order effects include an RPA community that is losing operators faster than it can train replacements, and a 5-year decline in the acceptance of the pilot retention bonus. There are no short-term solutions for these shortfalls. Full Presidential Budget (PB) 2016 funding, Overseas Contingency Operations funding moved to baseline, a reduction in deployment requirements, and time are necessary to develop the experienced Airmen required to repair Air Force readiness.

46. Senator KAINE. General Allyn, Admiral Howard, General Paxton, and General Spencer, what kind of impact would not only stopping basic training proficiency, but losing the opportunity to conduct advanced training, and what kind of impact that would have on our future generation of leaders?

General ALLYN. As codified in Title 10 US Code (Subtitle A, PART II, Chapter 39, Section 671), Soldiers may not be deployed without completing basic training. Initial Military Training (basic combat training and initial skills training) transforms volunteers into Soldiers with the requisite warfighting and technical skills to positively contribute to their unit. Without this foundational, institutional training, Soldiers would require burdensome, time-consuming training at their first unit of assignment. Additionally, standardization of initial training, when conducted at first unit of assignment, would be extremely difficult to ensure and lead to an increased risk of casualties in the event of a contingency. Delaying or halting the various advanced training courses offered to mid-career leaders will create a significant gap in professional development. This gap will force the Army to choose between placing leaders in positions of increasing responsibility without the appropriate level of professional education or delaying their promotion until such a time as the training can be completed.

Admiral HOWARD. Stopping basic training proficiency and pre-deployment advanced training would gravely impact the Navy's mission. We continually operate in a rotational deployment cycle, and the Combatant Commanders expect deployed Navy units to be ready to execute any core mission when and where directed. Therefore, full spectrum pre-deployment training is paramount.

If we return to sequestration, growing numbers of future leaders would develop experience gaps at key stages in their careers. Although Navy will prioritize pre-deployment training, sequestration will slow the training cycle. Non-deployed units will conduct advanced training ''just-in-time'' to complete deployment certification, and their post-deployment training to sustain readiness may not be funded. This reduces the total number of training opportunities at each career level. Joint partner participation in our certification exercises would also likely be reduced, and other cancelled or down-scoped advanced training exercises would limit the quantity and quality of additional training opportunities beyond pre-deployment certification.

General PAXTON. We are able to meet our current training requirements. However, in order to make continuous and long term readiness a reality, we have to strike the right balance between deployment for operations and training time here at home. Right now, we have about a 1:2 deployment to dwell ratio. That is, Marines are deployed for 7 months and home for 14. This allows a proper unit rotation to ensure that each time a unit deploys they are fully ready. If we are forced to take further cuts, that level will decrease closer to 1:1.5 or 1:1. What this means is that units have less time between deployments to conduct the required training prior to their next deployment.

More specifically, home station readiness is at risk when personnel and equipment are sourced to protect the readiness of deployed and next-to deploy units. This is a logical decision when validated operational requirements exceed resource availability. Home station units are expected to be in a higher state of readiness since the Marine Corps is charged to be the Nations' force in readiness. The way they preserve this readiness is through training. By way of example, 5 of the last 6 infantry battalions assigned to Marine Expeditionary Units were not prepared until 30 days before deployment. This is sufficient for planned deployments, but becomes problematic and dangerous as conflicts extend or the need to respond to unexpended crises arises.

To the point about our future leaders, it is essential that we have the ability not only to train leaders in tactical and technical skills at Professional Military Education (PME) courses, but also that those leaders have an opportunity to train with their subordinates during unit training. Cuts to either facet damage long term leadership development because leaders do not get the individual development they require and subordinates are not provided the opportunity to learn through interaction with seasoned and effective leaders. This creates a compounding downward spiral of competence and experience that we can ill afford.

General SPENCER. The loss of both basic and advanced training is reflected in the steady decline of overall Air Force readiness. The reality is that our current generations of Air Force Airmen have been heavily involved in low intensity or counterinsurgency conflicts for the past 14 years. Our Air Force, to include our leadership, is better than it has ever been at close air support, mobility, and special operations in low intensity operations. However, this has come at the expense of full spectrum readiness and the ability to fully support the Defense Strategic Guidance. For example, by 2012, 10+ years of cumulative skill atrophy have driven B–1 crews to routinely train for low-level attack missions at double the desired tactical altitude as a result of insufficient training proficiency and readiness. Simply put, the B–1 community sacrificed a distinct tactical and operational advantage due to fundamental aircrew safety and readiness concerns. A similar example exists in every Air Force community. Lost training has extended the matriculation of our future Air Force leaders. Lost opportunities to train and practice our ''high-end fight'' garner gaps of experience in our future leaders and insert unseen risk resulting in errors that will be swift and catastrophic.

Path to Full-Spectrum Readiness

47. Senator KAINE. General Allyn, Admiral Howard, General Paxton, and General Spencer, several of the Military Services have identified 2020 or 2023 as a target to restoring full-spectrum proficiency and address the degraded state of non-deployed readiness. Meanwhile, the Navy has an optimized fleet response plan to achieve consistent and long-term presence around the globe. In the event sequestration could be avoided—could each of you please describe in specifics how you plan to restore full-spectrum readiness and what the end-state looks like?

General ALLYN. The Army's readiness recovery goal is to build readiness for current operations and ensure enough operational depth is ready to sustain larger contingency operations.

The Army's ''get-well'' date is heavily influenced by two factors: demand for Army forces and funding availability. Assuming no change to current global demand and the fiscal year 2016 President's Budget (PB) funding levels are sustained, the Army forecasts achieving fiscal balance no earlier than fiscal year 2017 and returns to proficiency no earlier than fiscal year 2020. However, any increase in demand or reduction in funding will extend this recovery period. Fundamentally, we deliver full spectrum readiness through a combination of fully-resourced Home Station Training, culminating in a unit's successful completion of a decisive action Combat Training Center rotation. If fully resourced at current force levels, it would take two years to cycle all our active Brigade Combat Teams through this training regimen.

Admiral HOWARD. The Optimized Fleet Response Plan (OFRP) is the Navy's framework for readiness recovery. It is a disciplined process which preserves the time necessary to conduct required maintenance and modernization of our capital-intensive force. It also protects the time to conduct full spectrum training. Multiple lines of effort are being aligned to deliver the full readiness impact of OFRP. Achieving the desired end-state first depends on restoring the capacity of our shipyards and aviation depots. Our success will result in completion of maintenance and modernization on schedule; ready units that are available at sustainable levels from year-to-year to support Combatant Commander global presence requirements; and additional operational availability providing full contingency response capacity that is routinely sustained until the next maintenance cycle begins. Furthermore, to sustain full-spectrum readiness over time we must continue on a stable path to procure new platforms and ordnance, while also modifying existing platforms at a pace that sustains our warfighting advantage.

General PAXTON. Should sequestration be avoided and its deleterious pecuniary effects put aside, the Marine Corps recognizes that non-pecuniary actions and time would be required to restore full spectrum readiness. The Marine Corps is the Nation's ready force, a force capable of responding to crises and contingencies anywhere around the globe at a moment's notice. To fully reconstitute the whole-of-force after over a decade of sustained unprecedented conflict and fiscal challenges, the Marine Corps would continue taking actions that address readiness concerns across the Future Years Defense Plan. Those actions include: (1) *Balance readiness between deployed and home station units.* Forward deployed and engaged units will remain a priority for resourcing. However, to help lessen the burden of high operational tempo and improve overall readiness, the Marine Corps will employ deployment-to-dwell ratios that improve home station unit readiness. Personnel shortfalls at the unit level are a principal detractor to recovering readiness. Actions taken to help restore home station unit readiness include manning assignment policies that improve leader-to-led ratios, especially among the Noncommissioned Officer and Staff Noncommissioned Office grades; ensuring required unit personnel fill levels essential for combat effectiveness are protected; and that readiness recovery is optimized across the entire unit life cycle versus only the pre-deployment training period. (2) *Reconstitute the force to New Normal and upcoming challenges.* To meet current requirements and preserve readiness recovery, the Marine Corps will continue to mature its capstone concept and vision for designing and developing the force now and into the future. (3) *Equipment Reset.* Ground equipment supporting Operation Enduring Freedom has retrograded to the U.S. Much of this equipment has completed the required post-OEF repairs and subsequently has been redistributed to units. The Marine Corps is on track to complete repair and redistribution of all OEF war-torn equipment in fiscal year 2017.

For the Marine Corps, full spectrum readiness equates to Service-wide capability of operating, effectively and efficiently, across the range of military operations, and achieving mission objectives at any time or place. All Marine Corps units would be capable of responding to a broad spectrum of conflict scenarios. Full spectrum readiness allows the service to meet current and future requirements. Full spectrum readiness entails the ability to simultaneously meet (1) current operations supporting the Combatant Commands, (2) emergent crises and major contingencies, (3) the demands of the institution that underpins the ability to effectively and efficiently fulfill the Service's statutory and regulatory obligations.

General SPENCER. The Air Force is the smallest in its history and lacks the capacity to meet both the rotational Combatant Commander requirements and the required dwell time necessary to train in-garrison. With FY16 PB funding and a transition to deployment cycles that allow sufficient time to build and maintain full-spectrum readiness, the Air Force will be able to build readiness in the short, medium, and long term. Short term improvements will be derived from executing a robust flying hour program that emphasizes full-spectrum training. Mid-term gains are expected from accomplishing delayed maintenance and upgrades to weapon systems and support equipment. Long-term gains will come from investments in our Airmen. It takes time to recruit and train our Airmen to be journeymen, supervisors, and leaders who are ready to execute the full-spectrum of missions required of our Air Force. If 80 percent readiness is achieved by the end of 2023, the result will be a highly capable Air Force, able to meet the two largest pillars of the Defense Strategic Guidance with ready forces.

SEQUESTRATION RELIEF FOR OTHER U.S. SECURITY AGENCIES

48. Senator KAINE. General Allyn, Admiral Howard, General Paxton, and General Spencer, the new National Security Strategy released last month, states that our national security relies on more than just the work of Department of Defense (DOD). Sequestration is having as harmful an impact on our diplomatic and international development tools, Homeland security, law enforcement, and intelligence activities as well. Would you agree that we should provide sequestration relief to DOD and all the non-DOD contributors to our national security like the State Department, the Intelligence Community, the Department of Homeland Security, and the Department of Justice to name a few?

General ALLYN. There are several instruments of national power that we commonly refer to as "DIME" which stands for diplomatic, information, military, and economic. We are only one component of this—the remaining agencies provide the bulk of the other national capabilities. We believe that only through a whole-of-government approach can our national security objectives be met.

As such, it is our belief that even if sequestration relief were provided to the Department of Defense, the nation's ability to achieve its objectives would remain at risk without funding relief across the whole-of-government.

Admiral HOWARD. The Navy continues to oppose sequestration for the entire federal budget because it implements harmful automatic cuts with no regard for priority. The Navy is globally deployed to provide a credible and survivable strategic deterrent and to support the mission requirements of the regional Combatant Commanders. In executing our operations, the Navy relies on joint and interagency support from other DoD and non-DoD organizations. Any negative impacts to the organizations we partner with can have an impact on our ability to execute operations and the Defense Strategic Guidance. A return to sequestration would jeopardize the Navy's readiness and damage our national security.

General PAXTON. "While I do not dispute that national security is a whole-of-government effort, I cannot authoritatively comment on the potential impact of sequestration on any organization, other than the U.S. Marine Corps."

General SPENCER. Yes. Non-DoD agencies should be similarly considered for relief from sequestration. Any increase in defense spending should be matched at some level for the non-defense discretionary spending that contributes to our national security.

49. Senator KAINE. General Allyn, Admiral Howard, General Paxton, and General Spencer, if sequestration-level budget caps remain in fiscal year 2016, how would you characterize the impact of lost capability or capacity from these other agencies to meet the requirements of our Nation's security needs?

General ALLYN. The Army, and indeed the Department of Defense, cannot solely defend national security or meet the nation's strategic objectives in a way consistent with our values. The military is only one of the instruments available to the nation for achieving its objectives and securing its interests. Loss of capability and capacity in these other areas would certainly make our job more difficult and hinder the Nation's ability to meet its security objectives.

Admiral HOWARD. The Navy continues to oppose sequestration for the entire federal budget because it implements harmful automatic cuts with no regard for priority. The Navy is globally deployed to provide a credible and survivable strategic deterrent and to support the mission requirements of the regional Combatant Commanders. In executing our operations, the Navy relies on joint and interagency support from other DoD and non-DoD organizations. Any negative impacts to the organizations we partner with can have an impact on our ability to execute operations and the Defense Strategic Guidance. A return to sequestration would jeopardize the Navy's readiness and damage our national security.

General PAXTON. "While I do not dispute that national security is a whole-of-government effort and that sequestration could have an impact on the ability of other government organizations, I cannot authoritatively comment on the potential impact of sequestration on any organization, other than the U.S. Marine Corps."

General SPENCER. The Air Force relies heavily on the support of both DoD and non-DoD entities and will find it difficult to complete its mission if our agency partners lose capability or capacity. The support we receive through these relationships extends to all domains and strengthens our ability to conduct full-spectrum operations in support of our national interests.

50. Senator KAINE. General Allyn, Admiral Howard, General Paxton, and General Spencer, in your view, what would be the impact of sequestration-level budget cuts to Federal support services commonly used by soldiers, sailors, airmen, marines, and their families?

General ALLYN. The Army collaborates and coordinates with non-DoD agencies such as the Department of Agriculture, Health and Human Services, American Red Cross, Department of Labor and the Department of Veterans Affairs to achieve common Soldier and Family readiness goals. Non-DoD services and programs are an integral part of the Soldier and Family readiness system. Therefore, the readiness of Soldiers and Families who use non-DoD programs will inevitably be impacted by any reduction in outside agency programs or services.

From a strictly Army standpoint, Soldier and Family programs would be unavoidably impacted if we are funded at the Budget Control Act levels. We can protect the highest priority programs such as Exceptional Family Member Program, Survivor Outreach Services, Child and Youth Programs, Family Advocacy, and Financial Readiness for Soldiers and Families. However, there will be increased risk to programs such as spouse employment, Army OneSource, library services, and Family and Morale, Welfare and Recreation programs. Reductions will affect staffing, operating hours, and range of services, resulting in a potential degradation to readiness, resiliency, and quality of life.

Admiral HOWARD. Sequestration in fiscal year 2016 would have serious impacts to readiness overall. Because our Sailors are our most important asset and we must invest appropriately to keep a high-caliber all-volunteer force, we would try to minimize the impact to Sailor support, family readiness, and education programs. However, other support services may need to be reduced or delayed because of the significant funding reductions, which could negatively impact their morale and readiness. Furthermore, across-the-board sequestration cuts to non-DOD organizations such as the Consumer Financial Protection Bureau and the Department of Labor may also negatively impact the support services to our people.

General PAXTON. It is unclear how sequestration would affect the budgets and programs of other Federal programs. In regard to Marine Corps quality of life programs used by Marines and their families, recent budget reductions have already caused curtailment of many non-core programs, such as Family Care, Family Readiness, and Semper Fit and Recreation. We are currently protecting core programs, such as Behavioral Health, Sexual Assault Prevention, and Wounded Warrior care, as well as support services for Marines returning from Afghanistan and transitioning out of the Marine Corps. However, under prolonged sequestration-level budget cuts, even these programs could be put at risk.

Fundamentally, sequestration will exacerbate the challenges we have today including readiness of our Marines and their families including impacting the five pillars of readiness: high quality people, near unit readiness, capability and capacity to meet combatant commanders' requirements, infrastructure sustainment, and modernization. We have maintained near-term readiness at the cost of our long-term investments. The Budget Control Act has presented many readiness challenges and a sequestered budget would further exacerbate readiness issues.

General SPENCER. Under constrained budgets and impending sequestration, if not repealed, it is becoming more challenging to maintain diverse quality of life programs and services at adequate levels. The Air Force is committed to "Taking Care of People" and strives to maintain installation services and family programs to help build and maintain ready, resilient Airmen and their families. To help mitigate budget impacts, the Air Force has prioritized Airmen and family support programs from an enterprise-wide perspective. Our fitness, child and youth care, food services, and some family support programs (outdoor recreation, libraries, youth centers, etc.) are programmed to continue in the FY16 PB request. Funding below the PB request will force commanders to make difficult decisions to prioritize these support activities against operational and mission requirements.

51. Senator KAINE. General Allyn, Admiral Howard, General Paxton, and General Spencer, in your view, do reductions to federal support services hurt education and health care in local communities and ultimately risk the quality of life and readiness of our servicemembers and their families?

General ALLYN. Through DOD funding, the Army is maintaining a viable Voluntary Education Program IAW DoDI 1322.25 requirements. If funding to non-DOD Agencies (community and state schools) were reduced, it could have some impact on Soldier education by increasing costs not covered by the DOD programs.

Members of the Army and their families live and work in the communities surrounding our installations. While some members of the military live on installations with access to DoD schools, an increasing number (~80 percent of dependent Servicemembers children) do not. Instead, they use public or private education in the local community. Our members have access to military healthcare facilities in many locations but we still rely on local private and public sector healthcare services to augment our capabilities. Degradation of healthcare or education services within a community would impact the quality of life and readiness of our service members and their families.

Admiral HOWARD. Since the majority of our Sailors and their families live in the local communities surrounding the installations, if local community services are negatively impacted by reductions, our Sailors and families will likely share the same consequences with the local community. We have no data or feedback from regions or installations to substantiate negative impact on local community services.

General PAXTON. In specific regard to military and family quality of life support programs, we have taken cuts in areas of Family Care, Family Readiness, and Semper Fit and Recreation. As we move forward, we will evaluate our programs and develop a plan with a bias toward decentralizing decision-making and resource allocation. Funding will focus on sustainment of core readiness and higher headquarters requirements, such as Behavioral Health, Sexual Assault Prevention, and Wounded Warrior care. Marines and their families have and may be impacted by reductions in noncore programs due to accessibility of programs, establishment or increase of fees to use resources (e.g., youth programs, pools, etc.), and hours of operations (e.g., fitness facilities). However, the Marine Corps has made all efforts to find savings without resulting in direct impacts to our Marines and families and those impacts being minimal in areas of noncore programs. Funding reductions that impact support services do risk Marine and family quality of life and readiness, but it is not clear the impact on education and health care in local communities.

General SPENCER. Federal support services for education and health care, combined with Air Force programs, comprise the package of services that military families rely upon. Funding reductions for these programs result in less support to service members and their families. Many Air Force members and their families rely on public education and medical services available through local communities so reductions in federal support to these services adversely affect quality of life for service members.

AIRCRAFT MAINTENANCE THROUGHPUT ISSUES

52. Senator KAINE. Admiral Howard and General Paxton, with the delay of the F-35, legacy aircraft like the F/A-18 Hornet A and D models, must undergo service-life extension programs (SLEP) to cover the gap in aircraft coverage. In addition to sequestration-level budget caps, there have been reports of obsolescent parts, a shrinking to non-existent vendor industrial base, maintenance backlogs, and higher than planned failure rates as the aircraft age. Could you please explain how even if Congress were to give you additional funding, it may not fix the aircraft maintenance throughput issues, and how you either need relief from sequestration, decreased op-tempo, or more people?

Admiral Howard. The Fiscal Year 2016 President's Budget request provides funding to align F/A–18A–F depot throughput to projected capacity.

To improve F/A–18 depot capacity, the Department is attacking the major barriers to production—manpower and material. This includes an aggressive hiring and training plan for artisans and engineers, and improved parts availability and staging for high flight hour (HFH) maintenance events based on common repair requirements. Additionally, the Navy has collaborated with Boeing in identifying several areas to improve overall depot throughput, such as employing Boeing Engineering Support and incorporating Super Hornet modifications at its Cecil Field facility. The strategy is proving successful as depot production levels are improving, but requires time to fully mature. With the requested funding, and under this plan, the Department anticipates continued improvement in depot throughput to meet annual production requirements by fiscal year 2017 and full recovery by fiscal year 2019.

A return to sequestration in fiscal year 2016 is a recurring concern as the Department requires a stable budget to meet these objectives. Sequestration and the compound effects of the 2013 government shutdown drove manning shortfalls for both artisans and engineers and hampered the Navy's ability to respond to unplanned work found during HFH inspections. Any further reductions in the depot maintenance, engineering and contractor support budgets will impede the depot throughput improvement strategy. Moreover, a return to sequestration will affect recent initiatives including the F/A–18E/F service life assessment and extension programs (SLAP/SLEP). Current efforts for Super Hornet SLAP/SLEP include fatigue life analysis, stress predictions, and inspection and modification development. These analyses will inform future work and ensure material kits are developed to better support life extension efforts, but are required prior to the first aircraft reaching its 6,000 hour limit, expected in CY2017. A return to sequestration would have a compounding effect that will further increase risk in our strike fighter inventory management strategy and reduce the availability of warfighting assets.

General Paxton. The Marine Corps, along with all of the other services, is facing with issues with our current aircraft and keeping them relevant and ready while transitioning to new airframes in each of our aviation communities. The specter of sequestration-level budget caps frustrates the Marine Corps movement towards recovery and will reintroduce many of the problems from the first round of sequestration. Our Aviation Depots were not protected and we experienced a loss of skilled artisans and personnel. We are still rebuilding the workforce that we lost. It is critical that we do so to improve the throughput issues experienced with the SLEP and other engineering challenges we are experiencing with all of our type/model/series of aircraft: CH–53E, AV–8B, MV–22, H–1, and the more widely recognized F/A–18A–D. If given any additional funding, we would protect and grow manpower at our Depots to help with our Current Readiness challenges and increase our throughput.

In the near term, we are pursuing commercial alternatives as additions to our Depots to also increase throughput. This will directly translate to increased current readiness for all of our type/model/series of aircraft. We would continue to invest in our current fleet of aircraft to ensure their relevance on the battlefield as we continue to upgrade every aviation community. Finally, we would continue to fund our vital transition plan by purchasing more new aircraft in our current programs to complete our transitions sooner and divest of our current fleet faster, helping our Future Readiness.

The Marine Corps stands behind the fiscal year 2016 President's Budget and the Marine Corps' Unfunded Priorities List. This will help us keep all of our aircraft relevant and ready while continuing to build our F–35 fleet in addition to our other transitioning platforms. A return to sequestration would only exacerbate our issues with our aircraft, their modernization, and the SLEP programs necessary to make our way to aircraft like the F–35, CH–53K, and all other transitioning airframes.

Simulation Training

53. Senator Kaine. General Allyn, Admiral Howard, General Paxton, and General Spencer, the Chief of Nacal Operations' (CNO) Navigation Plan from 2015–2019 calls for focus on critical afloat and ashore readiness, including the "developing and fielding of live, virtual, and constructive training, to provide more realistic training at a reduced cost." For example, there is a 3–D software program called the Multipurpose Reconfigurable Training System (MRTS) that enables a sailor to view and access all parts of an engine found aboard Virginia class submarines. The Marine Corps uses combat convoy simulators at their bases in Quantico, California, North Carolina, Hawaii, and Japan. If we are unable to reverse sequestration, how can the

Services leverage simulators to maximize full-spectrum training proficiency in the face of fiscal constraints?

General ALLYN. The Army currently has the appropriate mix of live, virtual, and constructive training. The three complement each other allowing Soldiers to practice basic skills and in some cases to practice complex maneuvers prior to live execution. It is important to remember that virtual and constructive training cannot replace live training. Simulation allows for greater repetition and practice, but does not qualify a Soldier or unit as trained.

While simulations do save some training dollars, they are not a low cost solution. Simulating training requires complex and maintenance-intensive systems. The Army will always seek to optimize its investments in training resources, but there must be balance as some skills cannot be practiced in a simulator and units must execute live training to be proficient.

Admiral HOWARD. There remains a fine balance between the requirement for live, hands-on training and the complementary training capability provided by simulation. But even in a fiscally constrained environment, Navy is making the necessary investments to effectively leverage the live, virtual and constructive (LVC) training continuum to deliver more cost effective and higher quality training than live training alone can provide. New platforms, such as LCS, use simulation as the focus of their training, saving some of the expense of underway training operations, while we continue to invest in the Fleet Synthetic Training (FST) program, linking multiple Navy units, U.S. Joint Forces, and partner nations across the globe to practice operationally relevant scenarios. Current and planned investments will support our future training needs while continuing to improve the overall quality of tactical training.

Leveraging the successes we have achieved with FST and its connected tactical ship and aviation trainers, we are also applying simulation more frequently to maintenance training. The MRTS cited in your question is a good example. We are creating a virtual Virginia Class Submarine diesel engine room with considerable savings versus an alternative brick and mortar solution.

General PAXTON. There is no doubt that simulators provide a unique opportunity to provide realistic training opportunities that offset some of the costs associated with real-world training. These systems allow for varied training experiences, can minimize ammunition usage, and decrease logistical costs. In fact, the Commandant's Planning Guidance for 2015 specifically states that development and use of simulators remains a high priority for the service.

> "We will continue to support the fielding of systems that enhance our proficiency and safety in operating weapons and equipment. Our investment in training systems will reflect the priority we place on preparing for combat and be fully integrated with training and readiness standards. I expect all elements of the MAGTF to make extensive use of simulators where appropriate."
>
> -Gen. Joseph Dunford

However, as with other modernization efforts, we have had to defer some simulator development initiatives in order to prioritize near term readiness. We are currently funding simulator development and testing through individual system programs and supporting contracts. Due to the programming cycle, Fiscal Year 2018 will be the first opportunity to fund enduring integrated simulator capability.

Specifically, the Marine Corps Training and Education Command's (TECOM) Modeling and Simulation (M&S) Master Plan, Squad Immersive Training Environment (SITE), as well as the Live, Virtual, Constructive—Training Environment (LVC–TE) identify service requirements for simulators and simulations. These requirements are being addressed by TECOM. In conjunction with this we are continuing our efforts to integrate aviation systems with ground simulations to provide opportunities to conduct training that tests the full structure and capabilities of the Marine Air Ground Task Force (MAGTF).

General SPENCER. The Air Force is committed to ensuring force readiness in the most effective manner. Our combat and mobility communities, each have unique assets and therefore, different solutions. Some events/sorties can be replicated in the virtual world, while others cannot. In addition, for both communities, live training encompasses more participants than merely the aircrew. Maintenance, logistics, and airfield operations functions, to name a few, are active participants of the total flying activity and must be used every day to ensure combat power is available when and where the nation needs it. Current aircrew simulators do not exercise the entire logistical chain.

Air Combat Command utilizes simulators as an integrated component of a daily comprehensive live and virtual training construct. In conjunction with a command-wide realignment of the Ready Aircrew Program (RAP—the annual training specification) that occurred in 2010–2011, simulator training now constitutes 27 percent of total fighter RAP training, 40 percent of B–1 RAP training, and 50 percent of Command and Control, Intelligence, Surveillance and Reconnaissance RAP training. Given the quality and capacity of the combat simulators, there are not additional events/sorties that could be transferred to the virtual environment.

Air Mobility Command (AMC) offset over $700 million in live fly hours in fiscal year 2014 through the employment of Live, Virtual, and Constructive (LVC) capabilities. AMC has established a Distributed Mission Operations capability with networked connectivity for C–17s with other MAJCOMs and Joint partners to allow for expanded training opportunities in more realistic environments. AMC will expand upon current capabilities by connecting tanker (KC–10, KC–135, and KC–46) and additional airlift assets (C–130s and C–5s) over the next 5 years. In addition, AMC is pursuing a networked, virtual air refueling capability for their tanker and airlift systems to allow for additional migration of refueling training to the simulators (initial capability in fiscal year 2018).

[Whereupon, at 4:21 p.m., the hearing was adjourned.]